FIGHTING THE FEAR OF ENTREPRENEURSHIP

A GUIDE TO ASPIRING ENTREPRENEURS

ABHISHEK SENGUPTA

Contents

Preface

I realize that this book will be a great tool of assistance for the people who are think of starting a business. I have personally seen that starting a business faces a lot of roadblocks. Most of the roadblocks are just thmental ones. These are the blocks which stops a person from taking up business.

These hurdles are created out of ignorance and lack of knowledge about business concepts. Maximum percentage of aspirants gets stuck because of this. Lack of ecosystem and mentorship are the key reasons for this. I have described and explained each of the fear factors. Fear is a powerful force that can paralyze a person. It can also make you feel helpless when you are confronted with an unexpected situation. When the situation is not going your way, fear will make its way.

Here I have analysed the fear factors which a start-up founder face and reasons for that. I have made the approach scientific and easy to understand. I have even introduced some new concepts of business in this book. I have combined it ancient concept of "Navarasa".

My desire in writing this book was to a robust foundation for start of business for aspiring founders. This book is designed to have *powerful but simple-to-use business tools*. Using this book one can easily customize steps to suit one's needs and those of business.

The goal of this book is to introduce new age business concepts which will be of great help for business owners.

I have divided this book into three parts

1. Analysis of phobia
2. Dealing with phobias
3. Why people start business

This segregation will help a start-up founder to understand the concepts in a better way.

Analysis Of Phobia

CHAPTER I

Fighting The Fear Of Entrepreneurship

Fear of entrepreneurship is one of the most common phobias on earth. This is quite interesting. At some point of time everyone wants to start a business and live a life of his or her own. But could not! This is a common story. This story repeats. At the end of the story people leave the idea and manage the work for someone else's business in return of salary.

There could be different reasons for that. Everyone's life is different. Everyone circumstances are different. If we analyse the phobia, that gives some of the amazing facts. This we will discuss in the later part of this book. This has some deep roots in traditional form of society and education. Exact root of phobia is too tough to ascertain.

Every government in this world is encouraging entrepreneurship. This is a great step in long run. This step can be successful if people come forward and take up the challenge. This is a wonderful way to move ahead. Entrepreneurship has its own advantages. This can lead an entire new and better world. Entrepreneurship is a great and noble profession. Every product we use, in our day-to-day life is a product of entrepreneurship in some way or other. This is a great way for innovation. **Innovation and entrepreneurship are the two sides of the same coin.** Innovation needs to be supported by a strong sense of entrepreneurship spirit and vice versa. Entrepreneurship is a deep subject. This must be learnt to the fullest. Concept of this need, to be embedded inside the brain before the start. The embedded entrepreneurship spirit will help a person to make a head start.

With every passing day, the entrepreneurship is rising higher and higher. Many institutions have formed "entrepreneurship-cell" or "e-cell" to encourage the younger generation. This makes a favourable environment for the growth and development of entrepreneurship. Encouragement for this is done by many industrial bodies as well. Various programs are conducted for creating interest in young mind. Nurturing young mind in favour of entrepreneurship can be a boon for coming days. Moreover, the entrepreneurship is equivalent to more innovation. In turn, innovation is the need of the hour. In dynamic age of 21st century, innovation has to be encouraged to the fullest. This can be the real game changer. This can be possible with a touch of entrepreneurship. Regular 9 to 5 job - which I'm not discouraging - leave a near zero chances of innovation. **Human society, today need innovation in a huge way.** The human needs are changing and the new needs are emerging. Coping up with new needs is a challenge. Entrepreneurship is the only way to take up this challenge. This puts a step forward for entrepreneurship.

Everyone wants to be an owner of business, at some point of time in life. This is a great idea, but only handful of the people succeed to do so. This requires very strong mindset and requires a lot of knowledge about various business processes. Various skills like people handling skill, accounting skill, negotiation skills and strategy making skill etc are required for this. In other words, entrepreneur need to have a combo of all these. This makes many scared. But at the end of the day, this is an interesting and a challenging journey. So even after so many challenges, many people are so dedicated, that they take up the interesting journey of entrepreneurship.

At some point of time one need to take a call : how to make one's living? This question may seem familiar yet unfamiliar! But near to the end of the study cycle, this question emerges out in some way or other. Most of the time, parents put it across. By or before the end of the study curriculum, a person need to decide on this. By conventional way, people decide to take up job. Which is great! This decision is the by-product of our education system. Our education system is more inclined towards making a person, a good employee.

In some way, the lessons of leadership and entrepreneurship are missing from the curriculum. Remember, this is a completely different from management courses which are taught in various institutions. This drags all of us to one question: Is entrepreneurship a tough job ? This, I must say, is a relative question. Answer varies from person to person. If you ask me, I describe it as interesting but not tough. But many of my friends describe it as a tough move. So, this is a relative concept. Next comes the fear factors. Fear factors which result into phobias. I must say the fear factors are interesting ones. If you discuss them that will be fun. I have described them in the later part of this book. This phobia is even harmful for society as a whole. Phobias stop great work. Let's imagine if Mark Zuckerberg or Steve Jobs or Jeff Bezos suffered from these types of phobias, world would have been devoid of some of the finest products. Such phobias can even spoil any good work.

Phobias need to be dealt with. Right knowledge and mindset could be of great help. Such help can make phobias go away. Phobia is more linked to mindset and people around. This can be another pointer which require workout. Working out of these two parameters can help to a big extent. Most of the issues revolve around mindset.

Phobia is a usual response to many situations. At times, it is a normal human behaviour or response. Most of the time, it is a normal reaction. But most of the time problem, develop when it becomes a hindrance to work. Fear of entrepreneurship is one such phobia. This phobia stops one from taking up entrepreneurship. Acting as a hindrance is something which need to be worked upon. Hindrance stops many activities. These activities impart negative influence on one's brain. This influence acts as prohibiting force for all. Phobias need to be tackled with right knowledge and mindset.

CHAPTER II

Why Entrepreneurship Phobias Develop ?

Our traditional education system prepares of person for a good employee. This creates a deficiency of the "entrepreneurship stimulus". The reasons could be many. But they will help one person to hold his or her entrepreneurship dreams. Let's analyse some of the reasons.

1. Education System: Time and again, I have mentioned that the present education system do not make a person ready for entrepreneurship. The education system helps a person to become a good employee. The education system required thorough revision. Education system need to encourage innovation and risk taking. But in true sense, it does not make that. So, a person is not taught about innovation and risk taking - the 2 vital aspects of entrepreneurship. Hence, they fear entrepreneurship. This phobia is difficult to track. Here, the lack of knowledge is tough to handle. People avoid and fear, without knowing the right reason for this. By this, I mean, as two vital concepts are not taught in schools or educational curriculum. So, a profession based on those, is not seen as a lucrative career option. This thing gets engraved deep inside the brain of a person and in turn creates an opinion. This is too tough to assess. Formal education makes a mark on every person. So, it is the "impression of absence of a concept". Education system favouring entrepreneurship should be made in every country. This will flood the planet with innovation. The countries which have included these concepts in their education system are really making big impacts.

The curriculum has not changed much. Hence, too many new concepts are not included. So, the new concept of entrepreneurship, is not there in syllabus. This void creates an ignorance and ignorance lead to strange fears. This fear is stopping them everywhere.

Moreover, the system of education gives a score for consumption of knowledge. But the knowledge is also not refined and remade with changing time. Most of the contents of education are going on since ages. Change is minimal and turns towards a specific forum. Next comes "exams"!!! Examination in present day context, only determines how much knowledge one has consumed. This gives rise to many other stuff which run parallel streams like assuring better rank or entry to the next line of education. This system instead of adding creativity and preparing students for coming dates, adds to the stress levels of the students. Private tuitions, coaching classes, suggestion papers etc add more to the situation. This not only adds to the anxiety of the student but also adds to the stress of their family members. This gives no time and no scope to assess the interest level of the students. Further success is determined from the selection in higher education and the marks obtained. Many a times a person lands in the wrong profession, contradictory to his or her interest and expertise. So, this makes a person a part of just a "manufacturing unit". We are noticing many deviated behaviours among students leading to depression, nervous breakdown, addiction or even suicide.

Present day schooling is not made for tomorrow but for yesterday. This an unending activity trap, which need to be broken to see the new dawn. A dawn, where the student does not bend to find the shortcuts of getting good grades. This leaves a lot of gap and void, in our system. This void is a creating a sense of phobia of entrepreneurship.

2. Uncontent Society: In many parts of the world, society is not yet content. This causes or imposes too much stress on a person to start earning using the conventional methods and jobs. This may not be the case with many societies, but others do have this situation. This may leave a person out of innovation and risk taking - the two important aspects of entrepreneurship. If the basic needs of a family or a person are not fulfilled, the chance of entrepreneurship looks bleak. In such situation, primary target of a person is to fulfil them first.

Launching of business in an unconsent society is very difficult. Their rate of success is not known much, due to lack of data. But they may have the equal chances of success and failure. This is because a poor person faces same type of challenges as others face. However, the knowledge about the opportunities may be bit restricted for them. This creates a sense of fear. The uncontent society creates a sense of insecurity as well. This insecurity may be due to less or no contingency fund and adequate insurance. And uninsured society is more viable for insecurity. Such society most of the time lack innovation and risk-taking ability. It is technically tough to determine whether a society is content or uncontent. In developed countries the income that make society content is high as compared to underdeveloped countries. Low per capita income of a society further leads to situation leading to discouragement for entrepreneurship. This leaves a person with very less monetary security to take up any new or risky assignment. An uncontact society is too much engrossed with taking care of physiological needs. This leaves them less resources to deal with the new business. At times uncontent society is ignorant about new updates. This is primarily due to the consumption of time to gain and secure physiological needs. This leaves them with very little or no time for new business or innovative assignment. This situation is set to create a mental void. The mental void creates unwillingness or disinterest to take up a new business idea. At times, uncontent society is surrounded by many low-income activities and businesses. These are mostly small shops. Surrounded by many low-income businesses block the foresightedness and bigger ambition. They unknowingly get into an activity trap. This trap keeps going forever, unless someone takes courage and breaks it. For them a secure lifestyle could be getting out of their place and having an employment with the regular source of income. This again, stop them from taking up entrepreneurship. Many people from such situation get into earning from an early age. Most of them are even devoid of full education, which further stop them from taking up entrepreneurship activities.

Problems faced by them are numerous. This ranges from physiological needs, basic amenities, hygienic food, medical facilities etc etc. Many societies do not even have proper insurance to cover up their adversities. Under such situations, it is tough for them to think about a new venture.

3. Adverse opinion about business: Traditional business person impart a bad opinion in the mind of many people. They, at times, reflect a dishonest, tax-evading and unethically profit-making image. This is made based on some bad experience, other people's opinion, or even imaginary situations. But these create an adverse opinion for sure. These opinions, at times, are quite ironical. Many a times this may be a pure psychiatric situation. This may be self-imposed or may be embedded due to opinions of others. However, their opinion may or may not be true to the fullest. Most of the time, these opinions are based on half-truth and half-baked knowledge. After all, the little knowledge is a dangerous thing. But in this case, ignorance prevails. This makes the matter bit ironical as well. However, if we check the facts we will come know that all these points are completely different from what is painted. Entrepreneurs are one of the finest innovators. They pay huge taxes to the nation - much more than all other taxes taken together. Profit an entrepreneur generates gets served to the stakeholders in form of dividend, Government as corporate & indirect taxes and bonus to employees. Entrepreneurs also do a lot of CSR activities. These activities are huge service to the society. Many such activities at times create a big impact on society. Many such CSR activities did enormous work in field of education, healthcare, sanitization, etc. Gates foundation is well known for such work.

Once the knowledge comes, such misleading opinion get clarified. Now the government across the globe encouraging entrepreneurship. This will be great opportunity to eradicate misleading opinions. However, it can be a tough to deal situation with existing mindset. This cannot go off suddenly. This will go gradually. The change of mindset takes years and years.

In my opinion of phobia of new things, lead to an adverse mindset. What people do not know; their mind create a lot of unwanted stories. Let me explain this with an example. In olden days inaccessible places developed stories of evil spirits and ghosts. Just like this, an unknown or little-known work type gives rise to various adverse opinion and theories. Many, far from the truth, theories are generated like this. These are half baked and half cooked knowledge-based theories. Such situations go on from ages and stories are normal. Outcome of this types of theories are prohibition of next step of action. These types of theories mainly stop the next step. Here the next step is taking up all entrepreneurship. These mindsets take a lot of time to get rectified. These changes cannot be expected overnight.

4. Fear embedded in mind: Fear is a natural response or reflection. Fear is common in every person. This, at times, causes hindrance to future action. This can be another reason for fear of entrepreneurship. Fear embedded can be an inherited one from previous generations or can be developed owing to various circumstances. These are mainly psychological in nature. This can be countered with right counselling and knowledge. Right counselling can be beneficial not only for countering fear but also for facing such situations in future.

Finding the root of embedded fear may be difficult. These may or may not have a right reason. But any fear, can become a major hindrance to some work or other. Such fear needs to be checked with conscious efforts. Such efforts are too tough to execute, as it requires fight with oneself. Fight with oneself is quite tough. Embedded fear is tough to dismantle from the mind. Most of the time it remains in subconscious mind and appears and disappears with time. Subconscious mind is the part of brain which plays an important role in this. Nurturing subconscious requires difficult techniques. It's not controlled by conscious efforts. Such efforts control conscious mind.

Fear embedded in mind due to various reasons which most of the time cannot be pinpointed. So conscious efforts repeatedly can help to take charge of fear. But it may appear again, as I have stated.

One of the reasons of embedded fear, can be deep rooted superstition. Superstition are dangerous intuitions and stop anyone from taking up any new generation work. It makes people stuck with age old traditions. Many old traditions are scientific and beneficial, but many unscientific traditions are also prevalent in society. Such unscientific tradition gives rise to superstitions. Superstitions can be a by-product of disorder by the name of "obsessive compulsive disorder" or OCD. **Superstitions need to be treated with right knowledge and relevant practice.** Superstition also results in fear in the back of the mind. This could be one of the reasons causing hindrance to entrepreneurship.

5. Bad experience In past: Every person get a mix of good and bad experience during his or her lifetime. Good memories make a person cheered up whereas bad experiences make a person sceptical. Bad experiences impart a negative influence on the mind of a person. This negative influence works as inhibitor for many works. This inhibitor stops a person from a work or action. Bad experience may be self-acquired or injected into the brain by someone else. Whatever may be the reason such incident imparts a negative influence and this can be long lasting and long troubling.

Bad experiences affecting work are mostly psychiatric in nature. Such situations, most of the time fades away with time or conscious efforts. But in a small fraction of cases, such type of experiences live in mind. These start creating hurdles in many moves. With this, a person starts fearing many situations. Many new moves or an unknown move, draws them to onset of phobia.

Many a times some bad experience in past, stop a person from taking up entrepreneurship. This is more of a psychological situation. But phobia becomes real. Assessment of this phobia takes time and dates back to that incident. Most of the time the incident does not develop as full-grown phobia, rather it become a case of unwillingness. This case is totally different from phobia. This can be more taken as, lack of willingness or simply procrastination. That experience in past forms a stand in subconscious mind of a person. This subconscious mind plays with the decision-making ability of a person. Based on this, a person is not able to take any strong decision. Hence, this slowly develops into a phobia.

It is not difficult to counter this type of phobia developed out of bad experiences. A strong willpower and a positive mindset are important factors to counter this. Role of the mind and will-power plays a key role in this. But at times some bad experiences are too tough to deal with. Such type of experience requires professional medical help. However, such type of cases are little in number.

Every person at sometime or other, have or had a bad experience. Human beings most of the time manage the impacts of both good and bad experiences. They are part and parcel of one's life. Such experiences make a person and enhance his or her experience. So bad experience is a part of life.

6. One way flowing society: Society prefers one way flow. By this, I mean society is well a accustomed with ongoing ways of conduction. Anything going against the it, calls for an unusual trend. This mentality of an unusual trend-defining leads to phobias. This is true for the trend for business as well. If a society sees its member going on with a particular profession, any different professionals, will call for a sense of dissociation. This is the way leading to the fear of entrepreneurship.

If a society sees every member doing for farming and one person emerges to be a doctor, then out of the trend person creates fear for the society and trend-followers. Likewise, if the society is filled with 9 to 5 job people, and one emerges as an entrepreneur, it creates a sense of phobia. This phobia enters the mind of the family members and neighbours. It, then, slowly spreads to the whole society. This phobia develops due to unexplored path. **Path which are less travelled, creates phobia.** In ancient days people feared that earth was flat and the travellers might trip and fall from the edge of the earth. But once the travel started, this misconception slowly vanished. Society opposes a new step-maker. Whosoever make a different step is always countered by the society. This is a common scenario from the time immemorial.

Let me give another example: India's first practicing lady doctor, Dr Kadambini Ganguly. During that time girls never took the exam of medicine. They used to be confined inside the four walls of a house. They were meant for doing household chores only. During that time, she took a bold step forward and chose medicine. She was counted by the society at that time. Many faculties and fellow students too went against her. But she faced all adversities and came out as an example and inspiration for the whole country. These types of "anti-trend" phobias are common in all parts of the world. The lives of Jesus Christ, Lincoln, Gandhi, Mandela too saw the same.

Society always goes for one way traffic. Any deviation is taken as unconventional trend. These make society look on that person as "alien". In other words, it generates a sense of fear in the mind of general public. But an open minded and rightly educated society can come out of such dogmas and taboos easily. Open mindedness can be of great help in such situations.

CHAPTER III

Analyzing The Psychology

As I said, at some point of time everyone wanted to start something of their own. But most of the people fail to take their dreams further. This is a psychological trend, which keeps flowing. This is a psychological dogma which keeps going and going. This requires a deep analysis. Some of the interesting facts can come out with it.

1. Behavioral Inertia : Inertia, in physics, is defined as staying in a state. Law of inertia in physics is applicable to objects. But the law of behavioural inertia is applicable to human beings. A person is comfortable in staying in a pre-existing state and reluctant to take any new steps forward. This pre-existing state prevents a person from taking up business. Behavioural inertia is a deep-rooted trend. At times, this is difficult to discover. This is like a deep-water fish, which cannot be detected from surface. This is a hidden trend lying in the inner part of the brain. Behavioural inertia is quite common and sometimes adds up too many success stories. But problem develops when it prohibits someone take some additional steps. This becomes negative proposition in that case.

Behavioural inertia is a speed breaker. To some extent these are the results of lack of will power. Willpower has a lot of power. It can even make mountains move. This is a great tool. Willpower deficiency is a big trouble. This is more than a procrastination issue. This analysis needs to be done by oneself. Most of the time, detection of behavioural inertia takes time. This is because one's mind is unable to detect the problem at first level. Most of the time this is detected by another person. Even after detecting, realization takes time.

Behavioural inertia is more of a psychological matter. Lack of motivation can be another factor contributing to this. Motivation compels a person to come out of his or her zone of comfort. Lack of motivation can be a big contributing factor. In date to day course, the people slowly lose their motivation. This happens at snail's pace. This becomes equally tough to detect. Lack of motivation not only facilitates and contributes towards behavioural inertia but also prohibits many steps in life.

Behavioural inertia is a big problem. This stops a person in many ways. Not only in starting business, this even stops people in many ways in life.

Behavioural inertia is either contributed by people nearby or can be self-made. This starts to make behaviour deviated. This deviated behaviour can range from unwillingness to procrastination or even fearfulness etc. All these are negative trends. These negative trends impart negative influence in our mind. This affects conscious and unconscious mind. That in turn, generates negative vibes resulting in lack of action.

Analysis of the factors of behavioural inertia need to be done by oneself. This, at times, might seem like a frustrating exercise. But even then, this introspection is highly recommended. Factors contributing to behavioural inertia to be found and need to be pinpointed. This can help in sorting and correcting this and long run. This might take a lot of time. But what is important is to find the reasons contributing that.

2. Negative Self-Talk: Every person talks with oneself. This is a normal phenomenon. Self-talk needs to be properly done. Swami Vivekananda once recommended to talk with oneself at least one city. This will give a huge insight about oneself. Self-talk simply means talking with oneself. This is a great and wonderful for one's way forward. Self-talk needs to be rightly guided. Positive self-talk is beneficial for all whereas negative self-talk is destructive.

Fear of entrepreneurship or reluctant to start a business could have been an outcome of negative self-talk. As the name suggests this can help a person in positive ways. Negative self-talk is very harmful. Such type of self-talk doesn't allow a person to take up anything in life.

Negative self-talk makes a person negative. The mindset too turns negative. With this person start procrastinating. This kills innovation. This spoils the efficiency of work. This stops the process of knowledge gain. This lowers interpersonal skill. This makes a person demotivated. So, all negative trends start flowing. Slowly the person too becomes a person of negative mentality. Such a person is reluctant to take up any new assignment - starting new business.

Negative self-talk is of great disadvantage. Business do not accept people with negative trend. Business requires people with a lot of energy and positivity. Most of the time negative people avoid getting into business. Even if they get into, they quickly slip away. This is because they find themselves uncomfortable in that environment. Negative trends do not go ahead with challenging situations like business. In other words, such situation does not accept such person.

Negative self-talkers do not naturally get inclined towards business. So, in other words they avoid being in business. Their personality trends take them away from activities like this. So, the business is a process which attracts people of high and persistent positivity. So negative self-talkers do not have any place there.

So, starting a business is not considered as an option by such persons. In fact, not only business, they also do not pick up many other things. Such persons are, in their own cocoon and see problem in every solution. So, - solution to a problem - which is the real Moto of business is not a cup of tea for them.

3. Comfort Zone Addiction:Comfort zone is the real killer. Comfort zone is a zone in which people love to remain and unwilling to get out of it. Comfort zone prevents people to work. This is the real problem. This makes a person lethargic and lazy. This spoils efficiency as well.

Comfort zone is addictive. This makes a person addicted to it. This addiction is more dangerous than any other addiction. Coming out of this is quite tough. A fight with oneself is required for coming out. This is not so easy. This, at times, makes a person to reluctant to go for it. This addiction is a killer instinct. The addiction makes a person stubborn and a person of excuses. This puts a brake to all the things. Starting a business case, is one such thing which get the brake. Not only business, it puts a brake in almost all type of work.

This makes a person lethargic and lazy. This becomes a psychological factor. Laziness becomes a normal step in this. This delays any work. This delay spoils a lot of events. Such events are not accepted by the business processes. Hence, such kind of person get repulsion from business fraternity. The repulsion makes them run away from business. In other words, lazy and lethargic person cannot do business. Comfort zone is the real stop makers in business.

This factor reduces efficiency. Efficiency is the amount of work done per unit of time. With comfort zone coming in picture, efficiency takes a downward trend. Laziness and lethargy make less work per unit time. This reduces the efficiency. But businesses must run on high efficiency. Low efficiency games are not accepted in the world of business. Low efficiency means low production or outcome with high consumption of resources. This type of game is not accepted in business. Hence, comfort zone addicts are not accepted in business. In turn such people do not go for business. **Comfort zone also kills innovation.** Innovation is the prime requirement of business. Lack of innovation takes the business downward. Comfort zone addicts cannot come out of it, which in turn prevents them from innovation which is an indispensable point for business. People in comfort zone are too reluctant to take up any road which leads towards innovation. This finally repels them from taking up business.

Staying in comfort zone looks like a fun factor for them. They are happy in their own world. As a result, they cannot think of anything other than that. Sad part is, they pass on this phobia to nearby people.

4. Procrastination: It is a habit of delaying task. This is another hurdle in taking up a new task or business. This is more of a bad habit. This prohibits a person to take up any task. Habit of delaying makes a person mentally weak. A weak mentality person is too reluctant to do any type of work. This type of habit makes a person inefficient for work. The fall of efficiency is a killer for any business. Business is not a game of slow movers. They get rejected from a fast-moving business environment.

In other words, procrastinating person cannot make into such environment. Rather they fear such environment. Such type of fear is developed due to bad habit of oneself. This type of fear prevents oneself or even a person nearby to take up business. Most of the time procrastinators are rejected in any type of efficient environment. Not only business!!! Such people face a lot of hurdles in life. This is due to the bad habit which the person took up. This habit is bad for all types of works. This habit can take away all sorts of goods work gradually.

One of the reasons for procrastination is fear of not being successful. This is a sort of mental block. The mention of this is traced, centuries back. Greek philosophers like Aristotle and Socrates mention the world "akrasia". This is roughly defined as against the better judgment. This was used when a person has new the work but acted against it. This state is somewhat nearer to the state of procrastination. In other words, it is the force which prevents you from following what must be done. So, the behavioural irregularity was there since ages.

This is at times refers at time inconsistency. Let us understand it in simple terms. Let's take 2 hypothetical concepts one is **present time image** and the second is **future time image**. Let's take a job say - writing an article. Now let's divide this into above mentioned two images.

1. **Present time image:** Present time image of the job will be study of related topics, assembling the ideas, writing them, editing them and

finalising the article.

2. **Future time image:** This will include submitting the writeup and publishing that.

The link between present time image and future time images are required, to get the job done. Inconsistency develops when the link becomes snapped. If the future demands submission of the article but persons present time demand sleep, party or outings instead of article writing. As a result, the work gets postponed. Here, the situation of procrastination develops. Instead of following the present trends to get the better future goal, person takes up something else.

Procrastination is a big barrier and a negative trend. This cannot be compared with other negative trends like improper knowledge and laziness. This is more of a mental blockage. This mental blockage removal, need a lot of work out. This is a great fight with oneself. Root of procrastination can be many like inability to motivate oneself, low self-confidence, anxiety, negative thoughts, lack of ambitions, lack of interest etc.

Procrastination is self-defeating behaviour. This is a sign of weak personality. Such personality avoid taking a business for any other challenging work.

5. Dance Of Denial : There is a fine line of difference between procrastination and dance of denial. Dance of denial is denying the work with many unwanted or fictitious work. This situation can be defined as work on the desk but doing everything other than the work. This is a great obstruction to any work. Dance of denial is a hindrance in the start of business too. This is a great tool for not doing anything. This is simply a bad habit. A bad habit of avoiding work. Dance of denial makes a person inactive and unproductive. This not only stops a person from business but from many of the high energy jobs. This should not be confused with turn away of unwanted job. This is not avoiding unproductive job. This is avoiding productive jobs. This makes them reluctant to take up business or any other similar assignments. Such type of trends runaway from work. It is tough to analyse this trend. Many a times, just a bad mood make this. Many times, unproductive nature of a person makes this. Many a time confusion in decision making does this. Many a times simply unwillingness to do stuff, makes it. Like this exact analysis of the trend is quite difficult. Dance of denial is very much a destroying affair. This can destroy the productivity of any person. Loss of productivity makes a person unacceptable for any challenging work. At times, low productivity makes a person unsuitable for many assignments.

This type of dance is quite hazardous. This can make an assignment, a complete disaster. This disaster is too difficult to manage, at times. The dance of the denial is a spoilsport in all respect. This creates a peculiar situation, where in person knows what to do but avoids doing it. This mentality, if develops, while doing any hazardous work is well understood. But other than that, the action becomes tough to explain. Such type of situation even arises when anything uninteresting is presented to a person. Such type of situations, even arise in childhood days, when a child study all the subjects except the subject which he or she is not interested in.

Business is not so easy, although interesting. So many people start the dance of denial hearing this. So, this too stops them from taking up business. At times, this creates a fear factor in the mind of many people. In other words, it creates dance of denial.

6. Afraid Of Failing: Failing is a common thing in any assignment. Most of the time, any success is preceded by a series of failures. Failures are disappointing. But if you want to be an entrepreneur you must get habituated with failures. For most of the people, this is a fearful thing. This stops many from taking up business. Many known people tasted series of failures before success. Some of the failure stories can be learning lessons for many. One such story is of Col Sanders, the founder of KFC. He faced many failures before he could taste success. He failed in many ventures and did many odd jobs. But he kept trying. Finally, the KFC was born. Had he feared his failure, KFC would not have been in existence. Elon Musk too fail many times before success. Many known entrepreneurs failed before tasting success.

Entrepreneurship is a game of surviving failures. Here, the failures are much more than success. Only a fraction of attempts succeeds. This is a pure game of survival from failures. This is not uncommon. Many people face failures. These failures are heart-breaking. So here nerves of steel are required to face them. So, entrepreneurship is not a game for the people who are afraid of failing. If the people are afraid of failing, then it is not a suitable field for them.

Afraid of failure, may be due to various reasons. In spite of so many reasons, the game is tough and not suitable for many people. Many times, it is described as unsuitable for weak minded people. Different people might have different reasons for that.

This fear binds many people in their own comfort zone. Fear of failing stops a person from many tasks. Anything one do, there is always a chance of failure. This creates a fear in the mind of many people. This fear slowly gets bigger and bigger. Then the fear overtakes a person and stops from taking any step further. Entrepreneurship is a big step. Needless to say, that fear of failing stops a person from taking up this big step.

7. Decision Paralysis : This is a peculiar situation, wherein person fails to take a decision. This prohibits the person to take any step forward. As a person cannot decide, so he cannot make a move forward. This results in stagnancy. A person gets stuck. He cannot move forward or even backward. He gets stuck in the middle of the path.

Entrepreneurship requires fast decision making. But the decision paralysis stops the person from doing so. Hence, they cannot take up business. They ran away and leave the business. Quick decision making is one of the key requirements in business. But the situation stops the person. This delay may be dangerous for business.

This paralysis in decision making is dangerous in case of urgency or emergency. During those time, decision making need to be fast. But the decision paralysis makes it stuck. This can lead to a lot of damage or loss in business. Such loss can be hard to sustain. In business, urgency and emergency type situations are quite common. So, an entrepreneur needs to be quick to react with presence of mind. This is an essential quality required for business. This quality helped many entrepreneurs to come out of the difficult situations. People with decision paralysis cannot take care of such emergency or crisis. Such crisis handling is indispensable in business. Decision paralysis can spoil the whole game.

The people who suffer from decision paralysis are not fit for business or entrepreneurship. This creates a sense of fear, in the mind of such people. This slowly develops as fear of entrepreneurship. This makes steps backward from all types of work. This is one of the key contributors of the fear. Such people develop fear which has its root from many trends like this.

The exact origin of decision paralysis it's too difficult to find out. Many a times, this happens because of lack of knowledge, many a times it happens from lack of experience, many a times from bad experience in past, many times from personal reasons or even financial strains etc. But exact reason for this is too difficult to assess. Many a times procrastination is taken as one of the causes. Irrespective of the reasons this is a negative trend. Such trends can be a real killer during the crucial time. This is the reason why a business founder never have thisnegative trend. So, this trend makes anyone avoid business or related activities. For them business becomes scary to the core.

8. Lack of self-discipline: Self-discipline is one of the key criterion for business. All business founders need to have self-discipline. Many founders have specifically stressed on the self-discipline for business. There are many self-discipline trends in business like punctuality, quick response time, proactiveness etc. But people who lack self-discipline find it tough to deal with business environment. To many people, this gives rise to phobia. This phobia in turn repels them from business.

Self-discipline is a good and a positive trend. This helps many people in many ways in almost all types of work and all walks of life. Self-discipline helps to do many works in our life. But most of the people lack self-discipline.

This becomes a great quality. This quality becomes blessing for all. This leads to a lot of success stories in all spheres of life. Now the next concept is lack of discipline. Lack of discipline is a route to failure. This takes one away from success in the due course of time. This does not happen suddenly but happens over a period of time. This process is so slow that people fail to realise the shift. By the time they realise the deviation, it becomes too much to correct.

Many times, lack of willpower and lack of focus for the goal creates this. This is not created in a day. This is created slowly. This puts a bad impact on one's mindset. With bad mindset all bad thing starts rolling in. Exact reason of lack of self-discipline needs to be ascertained by the person himself. A self-introspection is required for this.

Many great personalities advocated the need of self-discipline. Theodore Roosevelt once quoted "With self-discipline almost anything is possible". He was true to the fullest. Robert Kiyosaki quoted "self-discipline is the number one delineating factor between rich, middle class and the poor". This is a great quality.

People lacking this quality find themselves uncomfortable with business or similar activities. Business or similar activities are high energy activities. Those in turn requires a lot of dedication and discipline. So, such people get scared of business or business like activities. Hence, they refrain themselves from this. They get a repulsion force from these activities. They either ran away from business or avoid it fully. This gives rise to strange phobia inside their mind.

9. Lack of persistence: Persistence is required in every walk of life. This is the key for success. There are many moments in life of an entrepreneur, wherein he or she suffers setback. These setbacks are demotivating moments. People trend to quit after such setbacks. That becomes the end of the matter. Here comes the importance of persistence. Persistence makes a person start again even after a setback. Persistent person keeps the whole matter moving. This is the key to beat setbacks.

People with persistence can beat all situations and come out of such setbacks. The power of persistence is quite huge. Bounce back after a failure require a very strong mindset. Such mindset helps to succeed in all walks of life. We know many people who failed in many attempts, but they kept trying and trying. Finally succeeded in their attempt. The famous failures are Thomas Edition's bulb experiment, Col Sanders's life, the life of Abraham Lincoln and so on. They all were persistent in their efforts, even after multiple failures and setbacks. For sure, this helps in their success. The persistent efforts not only overcome the setbacks but also overcome many hardships. This is a great blessing in life.

Journey of entrepreneurship is full of ups and downs. This is, at times, motivating and at times demotivating. But inspite of this one need to keep the work going. This quality is one of the indispensable qualities for entrepreneurship. Without this, one will not succeed. People lacking thisquality will not fit into the world of entrepreneurship. They will either quit or runaway. This gives rise and stand to face the unknown phobia in them. This phobia prohibits them from taking over entrepreneurship.

This development of phobia is due to anticipated projection in business. This takes those people away from business. At times, this demotivates and prevents them from taking business activities. This negative trend is not too difficult to study. Business is not a quick money-making option. Lot of hard-work and persistence is required. This phobia once developed, is difficult to dismantle. This is because phobia has origin from a negative mindset.

There could be another side for lack of persistence. This may be due to many compulsions. Many a times, situation on other hand has uncontrollable factors, which prohibits a person from taking another chance. This is considered as a situational factor; it is not a negative trend. This trend subsides once the specific situation diminishes. Many times, people who do not take the next step going to circumstances. But they take that next step, once the circumstances ease out.

10. Avoiding hardship: Every aspect of every work require hardship to the core. Hardship is the key to success. This is quite important. Hardship is the key to success even in business. This is quite important. During initial days of business, an entrepreneur does a lot of hardship. He or she has to do a lot of work to keep the business rolling. At times, number of working hours go beyond count. So, the hardship needs to be well planned.

The people who avoid hardship, find it difficult to enter the world of entrepreneurship. This is the reason they simply avoid this. Entrepreneurship is a work of hardship. This requires numerous sleepless nights, out of working hours schedule etc. Hardship is not only required physically but also mentally. Mental hardship is quite huge in business. Many a times, it becomes quite exhausting. But this is the real challenge, which is required for success of business. Hardship is an indispensable factor. More hardship a person provides more the business flourishes. The business stands due to the efforts by the founder and his or her team. We all know the stories of Dhirubhai Ambani - the founder of Reliance group, the Jeff Bezos - founder of Amazon, Colonel Sanders - founder of KFC. All those success stories are the preceded by a lot of struggle and hardship. These struggles create the success stories of various business empires. Another important name I must say is of Subhasini Mistry the founder of humanity hospital in Hanspur in West Bengal, India. Her husband died due to lack of treatment. On that day, she took a vow that she won't allow anyone to die like that. She sold vegetable to meets both ends. She sent her son to orphanage. After such hardships, she had put the foundation of the humanity hospital. Today it is a sparkling hospital treating patients with a very nominal fee. She was awarded by the president of India for her work.

Avoiding hardship is another negative trend. This prohibits many person from taking any challenging work, not only entrepreneurship or business. Negative trend analysis of this factor is very tough. This trend develops due to the bad habit or simply due to unwillingness to work. Too much analysis may not be required for this trend. This is mostly linked to improper mindset. Mindset is the key to counter this negative trend. So, the people who avoid hardship always avoid entrepreneurship. In other words, their subconscious mind develops a phobia - a phobia of entrepreneurship.

11. Lack of focus. Business work requires a lot of focus. One must focus on the real goal and avoid all types of distractions. This is the key for success in all walks of life. Focus, at times, is difficult to maintain. Today in the digital world there are so many distractions. Such distractions take the focus away. This focus needs to be properly kept at all types. Distractions to be avoided

Entrepreneurship require a lot of focus. A founder of business needs to focus on the business and its different aspects. This focus helps an entrepreneur to be in business. Focus is very vital aspect. Loss of focus can be a disaster in any work. Distractions are there at all places. These distractions prohibit a person from staying in job for a long time. These destructions take away productivity. They reduce the output per capita time. Such type of loss for productivity is degrading for any business. Loss of productivity increases the production cost. Moreover, the distraction can lead to mistakes and errors. Search errors can turn to blunder. Distractions even lead to accidents as well. Focus is really important.

Entrepreneurship is the game of staying in focus. People who are not focused cannot remain logged into the business. They runaway in the middle. Under all circumstances focus need to be in business. Lack of focus makes a person unfit for business. Trend of distraction makes a person avoid the run of entrepreneurship. This is purely due to the phobia generated due to mismatch of trends. Business requires this trend and people lacking focus has got different trend. So, this mismatch gives rise to the sense of phobia at the back of their mind.

As we analyse this trend, this may be due to a bad habit or even due to the psychological or mental disorder which we call as Attention Deficit Disorder or ADD. If this is due to the second reason, then the medical attention might be required. This could be followed by different prescribed therapies.

But if this happens due to the bad habit, then consciously controlling the habit makes a difference. Most common reason for this, is due to the electronic devices and digital media. Going to all this, can create a sense of fear. This fear gets into the mind and act to prohibit any type of positive or productive work.

12. Lack Of Planning: Planning is the blueprint of future action. This is one of the management functions. Planning is the seed over which the action depends. Benjamin Franklin, once said "If you fail to plan, then you plan to fail". That's the importance of planning. Nothing moves without a planning. Planning is the first step of management cycle.

Planning needs to be proper. Most important thing in planning is it has to be in written form. If the plan is not written, then it is of no use. The mental planning cannot be useful. You can of course do a mental brainstorming. But planning need to be on paper. This paper becomes a guiding paper for any job. This is an important trend for business. Without this business cannot move. Business will not even start without planning. Planning needs to be done first, then only any action will follow. Plan is the flow chart of all actions which need to be taken in due course of time. Planning is the real key. When the planning is not there, the scope of action gets limited. This reduces the real action to a great level. Reduction in the action reduces the scope of business. This is just a direct link in between. Written plan is a boon for business. Such written plan acts as a Bible. Next comes, the people who lacks plan. As I said, for business, planning is indispensable. People lacking planning, lack the blueprint for action. Now, if the blueprint is missing, the action is bound to miss. With missing action, the business will fall apart. Fall of a part of business, is equivalent to closure. So, the people who lack planning cannot take up business. Lack of planning slowly develops into a phobia. This fear prevents many challenging works. Entrepreneurship is one such challenging work. This becomes the barrier.

Analysing this negative trend is not tough. Most of the time, this develops due to lack of discipline. Lack of discipline makes the habit of not planning. In other words, what is the result of this bad habit. This develops, at times, due to improper mindset as well. Right mindset helps to build the right habit and vice versa. Improper mindset gives rise to many bad habits. Keeping right mindset is quite important. This bad habit can be a by-product of procrastination as well.

Whatever might be the reason for this. This negative trend makes one unsuitable for almost all challenging tasks. Every assignment requires people with right planning and right organization. Remember an organization can only succeed if the planning is right.

13. Unorganised activity: Many people take up business as a quick money-making game. When you take this, saying so called side business for getting some quick bucks. This is illusion, there is no such concept as side business. Such part time works not businesses. These works are mistakenly termed as business. Such activities just gigs, or results of moonlighting. Those maybe pocket money-making activities. Many people take up those, mistakenly thinking as business. Unfortunately, these activities are not organised once. They are not regulated as well. Unorganised and unregulated activity do not have long prospects. These activities are not even compliant to the laws. So, the credibility of such activities is a big question mark.

Business is an organised effort. Such efforts are commonly channelized as per the documents of business. All activities of business must be compliant with the laws of land. On the other hand, so called petty activities, are not at all organised or compliant by laws. Such activities are not credible. These are generally not regulated by any authorities. Many people take up those activities and call those as business, which is not. So, here they either get cold or face loss. At times, they earn as well. Once they fail, they quit the process. And after quitting they develop fear. Most interestingly, they start preaching their experience to others. The fear spreads like that.

If we analyse this, we will see such things developed due to ignorance and lack of guidance. If the person would have been knowledgeable, he or she would not have taken such unorganised activities and considered those as business. Business requires guidance and mentorship. Right guidance for mentorship can prohibit taking such activities. In other words, these are the acts of ignorance.

So, unorganised activities generate the fear factor. Such fear factors travel from one person to other. These factors are quick to spread and goes around and around. Such wrong stuffs spread a negative aura. This aura is quite powerful. This aura of negativity prohibits people from taking up any kind of positive work. This event even takes them backward.

14. Quick money-making expectation: Many considers business as a quick money-making game. This is a misconception. Business is not like that. This is a long-term game. Profit gets reaped in long run. People need to nurture the business. It is like, raising a child. A child needs to be raised with due course of time. Slowly with time, business gets better, and crosses break even. Then it starts generating profit. It is not it easy to touch the break-even point. At times, it takes years after years. So, a person must be patient till that time. Right strategy and right book-keeping are the key.

Just to indemnify, business is not a lottery ticket. It is a long-term investment. Investment will take time to yield results. This never happens overnight. If anyone makes any claims of making quick money, my suggestion is to stay away. This cannot be the reality with ethical ways of business in place. So, the right knowledge about the business is required. This will have the clarity of business processes. Businesses is all about making money in long run with the growth of business. So, the "lottery mentality" need to be abandoned. This is not a real concept. This concept must be taken off the mind. No one can become a business tycoon overnight. It requires years of hard work. After years and years of grinding and hustling, a business becomes profitable. This is a hard reality. Remember there is no shortcut to success.

People who think business is a quick money-making opportunity, their opinions must not be considered. They generally enter business and after seeing the hardship, they are eager to dissociate themselves. They become eager to leave the business. A fraction of them, also get into unethical ways of business. Both are negative situations and are quite disastrous for business and for the founder.

Such type of ignorance creates a phobia. Phobia travels from one person to other. This is a strange situation. Such situation is purely due to wrong perception and ignorance. Right perception about business can clear the cloud.

So, do not think business is a quick money-making option. Such options do not exist. Money in business comes with time. This info needs to go deep into the brain. Never enter a business with a quick money-making mentality.

15. Lack of knowledge: Knowledge is one of the key criteria in business. Business is an option for the people having the right knowledge. Right knowledge can lead to the things going further and further. One of the basic reasons why people fear the business is due to improper knowledge. People with right knowledge always know the subject and become perfectly suitable for business. Now lack of knowledge or improper knowledge leads to development of such kind of phobia. This is the problem which keeps developing and spreading. This problem will keep spreading unless the light of knowledge is drawn.

Lack of knowledge is one of the dangerous aspects of business. Other dangerous aspect is, half-baked knowledge. Second aspect is even much more dangerous. This aspect even spread lot of rumours. Such rumours made from half-baked knowledge is quite dangerous. Business is a vast subject. This requires a lot of study. Most of the people do not do much study. Instead, they believe what others say. Most of the time they know a little. Hence, the cycle of ignorance goes on. This spreads and make rounds as interesting gossips with half-baked truth. People need to identify the truth from the half-baked ones. Such gossips need to be countered with right knowledge. People with lack of knowledge are negative trend spreaders.

Lack of knowledge gives rise to various types of superstitions and ignorant activities. Such things are the obstacles to any work. These obstacles spread by the word of mouth and the impart a negative influence on anyone's mindset. Negative mindset is an instrument of trouble. Such trouble creates a shadow of phobia on a person. This is very tough to handle as such persons do not have knowledge to counter the negative situation. So, clearing mindset is too tough for them.

So, lack of knowledge imparts a dark cloud on any assignment including entrepreneurship. This makes entrepreneurship full of doubt and confusion. This makes the step difficult as a strange fear develops in the mind. This fear prevents further and marches towards fear of entrepreneurship.

Getting right knowledge about entrepreneurship is the key to counter this. Remember entrepreneurship is a vast subject. That's why mentorship is recommended for this journey. Right hand holding is the key.

16. Deviated mindset: Deviated mindset is difficult to explain. This mindset is either influenced by bad influence or extreme lack of knowledge. The sometimes becomes quite dangerous. Mindset rules the action of a person. Right mindset defines the right action and vice versa. So, if mindsets get deviated then that deviated action starts taking place. Mindset do not take up any challenging or positive assignments. They will not only fail to take up but they even discourage others.

Or deviated mindset can occur due to many reasons. Results may start from addiction, bad influence, drugs, political influence etc. Such type of influence can make the mindset deviated. In reality, the mindset goes away from reality. At times, mindset cannot accept the reality. Such mindset can even be hard on society and other people. Such type of mindset is tough to assess.

A deviated mindset can develop from influences. Influences can range from a bad thought to political corners. Such types of influenced deviated mindset stop all sort of activities. Such situation develops when the brain failed to distinguish between good and bad thoughts. With a bad thoughts keep going in the brain without any barrier or correction, right mindset gets defeated. Such type of mindset develops a hatred towards a section. This section can be of business as well. Hatred in form of deviated mindset slowly develops into action. Which leads to opposing to many things. Deviated mindset under the influence is a great disaster.

Such the deviated mindset can be harmful for entrepreneurship. Such mindset not only makes a person stop work but also stop others as well. The spread of negativity is quite common. Such a way is very harmful for society. So deviated mindset needs to be identified soon and tackled properly. It generally starts from one person or a small group and start spreading. Such spread can only be checked with the knowledge and fact-finding exercise. Most of the time such mindset developed due to the wrong fact or certain way of presenting a fact. Hence, all type of fact presentation needs to be checked and fact finding must be done. Also, the presentation of the right fact in front of the public becomes necessary.

CHAPTER IV

Analyzing Circumstances

Let us analyse the circumstances based on which people avoid entrepreneurship. In the last chapter, I discussed and analysed the psychology. Circumstances are somehow similar as psychology but is bit different. Circumstances are the situation with stops a person. These circumstances are the factors using which people take their decisions. These are vital ones.

Circumstances can be the result of self-made situation or might come up as a result of certain unplanned scenarios. These situations, then become a deciding factor for any future action. Circumstances influence the decision. Here, it won't be right to say anything as right or wrong unlike the psychology chapter. The analysis of circumstances is different as every person's life is different.

These circumstances make a person to decide their next move. So, these types of situations are the deciding factor in the life of people. It would be wrong to analyse a person based on situations. Many a times, it is decided by external factors. In other words, decisions make the situation. So, the situation may be specific to a person. So, the circumstances become the key factors for decision making. Such factors are the results of many factors taken together. Multiple factors contribute to specific factor. Circumstances can make decision. Circumstances have head on both sides. It can lead or it can lag. This is the real key. Many times, people say they drop their plans due to circumstances. So, here the right analysis of circumstances is required. This chapter can be beneficial for the people who want to know and deal with the situation. This makes the decision of life. So, knowing and analysing circumstances is important. This may be tough as circumstances are too difficult to analyse. So, making a note of circumstances. These matters impart a lot of influence in one's life. So, the first thing one need to do is identify the circumstances. This makes the way to know and deal with it. Main issue comes because people fail to identify those. One need to do this properly.

1. Lack of risk appetite

Everything or every action in the world involves a certain risk. This is nothing unusual. This is a universal phenomenal. People take up various jobs based on their capacity to take risk. This is called risk appetite. So, every action of a person is directly dependent on the risk appetite the person has. Risk appetite of a person determines his or her actions.

People with risk appetite can take up many assignments. Business is one such assignment. This requires a lot of risk appetite. Risk appetite is an important criterion for taking up business. Risk taking is at times the deciding factor. It would be wrong to assess a person over risk appetite. That's because everyone's life is different, and everyone's situations are different. Situation determines risk appetite.

Business requires a lot of risk appetite. Every start is a risk. Every start has equal chance of success and failure. So, this has equal risk every time. So, this risk needs to be checked before start. This finding needs to be analysed well. This analysis will be analysed. Then the same is well calculated by business founder. This calculation determines risk taking ability of founder. This is also a psychological game. This is a game which can be played with organised approach. This screen can be played with the right mindset. Mindset makes a game changer. Risk which a person can take depends on his or her psychology and mindset. These are two strong factors. A strong mindset can take a higher quantum of risk and vice versa. This factor plays a role in taking up business and starting entrepreneurship. So strong mindset is a great thing for business.

Risk requires thorough analysis. First thing to check is what is the quantum of risk involved in the work. Higher the quantum higher is the risk involved and vice versa. An aspiring entrepreneur need to analyse this. Based on his or her analysis, they can decide on the proposed assignment. This assignment taken up is based on the risk-taking ability of the person. Risk of business is just like any other risk. But this is termed as a risk due to the fear of failure. This makes the business an affair of risk. These need a deeper thinking. Every success is preceded by episodes of failure. Many entrepreneurs succeeded after failing multiple times. These are real sources of inspiration. This is the call of entrepreneur. This is also the test of aspiring entrepreneur's risk-taking ability. This is the first situation which need to be assessed. These circumstances are not uncommon. Every new assignment requires an appetite of risk.

If the risk appetite too low is a problem and risk appetite too high is also a problem. An aspiring entrepreneur need to find the optimum point between those. Low risk appetite prevents a person from taking any new assignments. At the same time, high risk appetite tempts a person to take a risky assignment. So, risk appetite at the right level makes a difference.

Despite all, analysing risk appetite of aspiring entrepreneur really matters. This appetite marks and decides the intention of start. So, this becomes a deciding factor for the start as well. This is the factor of starting. This decides whether an aspiring entrepreneur will take up the assignment or not. So, this is the first circumstances one need to see and analyse.

2. Liabilities

Liabilities slowly becoming a part and parcel of life. This feature is bit tough to explain. Liabilities maybe wanted and unwanted both. Liabilities, at times, come up as an instrument to overcome many uncertainties. These liabilities, if not managed properly, leads to utter distress. This happens with everyone. Liabilities are even taken to manage lifestyle standards. This is bit disturbing and totally discouraging. This may lead to too many liabilities. Generally, liability comes in form of loans, debts, overdrafts, credit card usage etc. These, if not handled properly, can lead to bad financial status. If a person is not financially stable, he or she cannot take up a new assignment. This is a great hindrance. This is not a great step.

Business is a great challenge. So, this challenge cannot be taken with liabilities on hand. Liabilities if not managed can stop a person from taking any business assignments. This is too tough and at times takes time to deal with it. Liabilities cannot go off in a while. This takes time and patience. This is a great struggle. Liabilities stop a lot of things in life. This takes a person backwards in life.

At times depth are taken for expansion of certain businesses related things. A school of thought says that debt is good. There is another debt which doesn't yield anything, rather eats up percentage of income. So, the debt of later type is considered as full borne liability. This liability plays an inverse effect on the person. Many times, people get into debt to purchase what might not be required. This is a behavioural malfunction. This need to be checked through various conscious efforts.

Many times, in order to maintain the lifestyle people, get into debt. This type of depth is a killer. Once a person gets into debt. They enter into an unending cycle. This most of the time keeps going and going. Very few people came out of this. This cycle is terrifying. Liabilities are not only debt. But the debt is one of the most common liabilities. Another popular liability is overspending. People spend more than they could afford. This is another habitual issue. This is more of a habit than anything else. This leads to more liabilities in one's life. This is a great downward trend in life.

For liability hit person, it is impossible for a person to take up assignments like business. This makes a person fearful. This fear stops a person. The fear is very dangerous as it holds a person from the next move. Liabilities can make a person totally handicapped. This is not uncommon. Many people take up unexplained and unplanned liabilities. This liability acts as a hurdle in many ways. This fear factor is quite common in the people with liabilities or debt.

Many things cannot be taken up due to the fear arising out of liabilities. These are the real wall between a person and the dream business. This obstacle cannot be removed easily. Obstacle remains for a long time. This is a financial obstacle. This type of matter requires a lot of planning and the time to sort. So, this is one important factor which create the fear of entrepreneurship. This stops a person from taking up entrepreneurship.

3. Lack of experience

Many claims lack of experience as a reason for not starting a business. This is very common reason. This may not be a real reason. Lack of experience is difficult to count. Many times, people claim that their previous generation didn't do business. So, they do not have experience. At times people claim that they never did any business in past. At times, person claim that neither his or her family nor friends ever had any business. Pointers go on!!! Lack of experience slowly becomes a hindrance.

Experience may or may not be a hurdle. There are certain business which requires certain basic knowledge to start. However, in almost all businesses, learn as you go mode plays a role. Most of business founders have no or very little experience. They start business and slowly gained experience. So, the lack of experience concept might not be a big issue. Many "on the go" experiences are available in business. Many "on the go" lessons are available as well. With every passing day new experiences and lessons can be learnt. This is a common trend in entrepreneurship. Experience is not always a proceeding factor for any work. Especially for business! Experience prior to start may not be a deciding factor at all. Technical and basics of business are required at times. Experiences are gained with passage of time. Experience of two persons operating similar businesses can be different. Some may have got good; some may have bad. Experience cannot be engineered or purchased. Those need to be learnt. Those must be gained. So, experiences comprise of many factors, situation handling, problems handling, tackling crisis and celebrating success. This is a great learning which happens overtime.

Experience is a great instrument. One cannot expect a person too become experienced, before starting a business. Every step of business lead to addition of experience. Experience is ever-going process. This is a gradual process. With every passing day experience increases. This enriches a person every day. Always remember an experience person was once an inexperienced one. He became experienced after years of hard work and learning. This process takes time. One need to be patient with it and start. Many big stalwarts of business were inexperienced and were the first-generation entrepreneurs at one point of time. These first-generation entrepreneurs did not had any family experience before they made their own roads. There are many known names. Bill Gates, Steve Jobs, Mark Zuckerberg etc are some of the examples. These names must knock your brain. They too didn't had any experience. But they created business empires of their own. So, lack of experience is more of a mental factor and a mental block. The basic knowledge is the thing which is required but experience is one aspect which develops over a period of time. So, experience at times takes a decisive stand for business but might not be block. So, this must not be given too much weightage for the start of business. There are many ways that these can be tackled. Right advisory and mentorship can compensate for the experience. The startup founder may not have experience, but mentorship and right advisory can be of great help to compensate that. So, the people get stuck claiming the lack of experience which may or may not be the right point.

4. Discouragements

Discouragement by near and dear ones to prohibit a person from taking up entrepreneurship. This discouragement, which flows from near and dear ones, stop many people from taking up business. This discouragement might happen due to the fear embedded in their mind and eventually flowing out discouraging others.

If we analyse this bit deeper, such discouragement comes from people who are inexperienced. Proper experience people will never discourage rather they will have the right advice for others. So, the discouragement comes from the people with less or no experience. Discouragement also flows in from ignorant people. Right knowledge can clear the air of confusion about entrepreneurship. Lack of knowledge creates an atmosphere of ignorance. This ignorance creates and spreads more ignorance. This is another negative factor. This is not a factor to stress upon but a factor to ignore. This is a factor if faced by someone, then the person needs a thorough mental revamp. It is necessary.

This spreads a lot of negativities. Most of the time it comes in form of unsolicited advice. Such type of advice come from all corners. This is a negativity spreading factor. Negative factors keep hitting the subconscious brain and retards the decision-making ability of a person. Negativity gets inside a person with all type of negative aspects. This stops a person from any forward decisions. This imparts negative influence in all spheres of life.

Discouragement happens in all spheres of life. This imparts negative psychological impact on many aspects. Discouragement is a major negative influence maker. This stops many assignments. This works as a great hurdle. This hurdle makes the opinion of others. This opinion imparts a psychological impact for a listener. This plays with the mindset of the person. Positive mindset is a boon whereas negative mindset is a curse. Discouragement is instrument for making negative mindset. This type of mindset keeps lingering for a long time and keeps finding trouble in every move.

Dealing with such discouragement is not that tough. This can be dealt by avoiding discouragement done by listening to selective advises. Many advice flow in from various corners. So effective hearing is the key.

There is another type of discouragement. I call it as action-based discouragement. In this discouragement, people around us, create hurdles. This is done so that the work does not happen. So, such actions are negative actions. This can be even harmful at times. So, dealing with action-based discouragement is bit tough. Both advice based and action best discouragement need to be fought.

This is common in all societies across the globe. This is a negative trend which keeps going. This negative trend is like any other external factors, which imparts negative influence. So, this has to be dealt with proper ways. Discouragement at times can be depressing as well. This is a great hurdle in any new work.

So that discouragement needs to be well tackled. One must not get depressed with discouragement rather must fight out with courage

5. Lack of funding or capital

Funding or capital is one of the basic requirements for business. This, at times, might become a deciding factor. If someone is opting for a service business, then he or she can manage to start or run a business with the right cash flow management. But if someone want to set up a factory or manufacturing unit, then he or she might require fund or capital. So, the lack of funding or lack of access to the funds, might lead to hurdles in business.

This depends on the type of business and the industry type as well. This is the thing which makes a person slow due to availability or non-availability of funds. This at times matters.

People who have knowledge and access to funding are more likely to start a business as compared to the people who do not. The countries where the seed funding is readily available sees a huge growth of start-ups and vice versa. This at time creates a difference. Making funds readily available is a challenge, specially, in the developing countries. Developed countries most of the time have will established funding systems.

Funding is available at many places in some form or other. Funding knowledge is important. Just knowing the source of fund is not going to do anything better. One need to know the processes, details and eligibility criteria etc. In depth knowledge of the whole process of funding is the real key. Many times, an aspiring entrepreneur might not know the full process. There lies the issue. So, the circumstantial issue is created here. This takes a bit away from the journey and develops a sense of phobia.

This phobia may be due to lack of knowledge or lack of right connect. This may be a temporary factor at times. Such factors may vanish after the knowledge is acquired or the right connect is opted. This may be taken care with the right hand holding and mentorship. Still, these factors become prominent with many people who would like to go for production or factory setup. This is a hurdle, at times.

Phobias develop when there is a lack of knowledge. Lack of knowledge facilitate distorted thoughts in brain. This gives rise to the various phobias. Most of the phobias are the virtual creations of mind which hardly has got any significance in real life.

Lack of funding can be termed as a hurdle instead of phobia. But, the people still consider it as a phobia. Hurdle and phobias are two different meaning words. This can easily be sorted with the right guidance. This funding solution can lead to evolution of many budding entrepreneurs and start-up founders. Lack of funding is a hurdle, of course, but may not be a fear or phobia. So, right handling of the situation can counter this point quite well. This hurdle is quite common amongst the budding entrepreneurs. Many institutions, governments and mentors are coming up to assist in this point. Now a days, lack of capital is getting countered in well organised way. There are many examples where a start-up founder got assistance from various incubators to overcome this hurdle. This is helpful for the start-up journey with the passage of time. Start-up journey will get easy with more access to funding. So, the right approach matters. Approaching right person or institution can solve the issue and remove the hurdle. So, consider this point as a hurdle not as a phobia.

6. Complicated process

Starting a business is a process-based job. This involves a lot of processes. This at times may seem like a complicated one. But it is not. Right hand holding and the proper guidance is the key. This can be eased in a numerous ways.

Business involves a lot of paperwork. This is a specialized job. This requires proper guidance from the professional persons. This may require external help as well. I must say the process may be bit tedious but nothing to worry about that. This is just one of the many processors in business. Paperwork is important for any business as it gives a touch of authenticity and compliance to the company. In long run it will earn the trust of the client. Processes are important for that.

Most people get fearful with the business processes because of ignorance. Lack of knowledge generates the fear factor. The fear factor acts as a hurdle and hindrance. This may be cleared with the right knowledge and the flow of information. This is a great way to overcome phobias. But, at times, half an unbaked knowledge, too cooks many fear factors. This is one of them. Business involves many processes. This may be one or combination of many processors. These processes vary from country to country and industry to industry. But the processes have to be what it is assigned by the rules of the land. This is the thing one need to know before the start of business. The processes of business are the strength of business. Correct process makes a business perfect. The right process certifies the credibility.

Paperwork is a great asset for any company. This is the process which makes the way for statutory and compliance related processes. This makes many people nervous. This nervousness is quite normal when it comes to aspiring entrepreneurs. This is common in almost every part of the world. So, everyone who built the business made the paper works and gone through the same process. This is the regular path for the journey. Many travelled before, on the same path. This makes the business. Rather that is how a business gets born. This process can be eased out with the right knowledge and hand holding. So, this is a regular way.

Brighter side of the processes is that it is it gives a company a proper legal entity. Legal entity is important for functioning of the company. At the same time, it develops a sense of credibility amongst stakeholders. This credibility gives rise to a factor of trust. This trust becomes the best stand for any business. No business goes on without trust. Customers who do business with a company only when they have the trust. Customers do not pay for the service or product, rather pays for the trust factor. This factor develops only when a company follow proper processes and secures proper paperwork. Without those, business units do not take a proper shape. Improper company is not liked by any customer or stakeholders.

Processes may be complicated, at times, depending on the type of business. Many types of business are easy to make, whereas certain are tough to do. So, before start, the business type must be well researched along with the formation process and required paperwork. Needless to say, knowledge and hand holding plays an important role.

7. Fear of unknown

Business journey is quite undiscovered one. An entrepreneur explores the journey of his or her own. This journey goes, as one moves with it. Result or destination is not quite visible at start. This creates a fear of unknown with many people. So, this is another circumstance, which stop people from joining the journey of entrepreneurship.

This fear is quite common with most of the people. As comparatively a smaller number of people take up business. So, the journey of entrepreneurship is not well known to the general public. Hence, advance journey steps are not much known. This creates a psychological vacuum in the mind of people. This vacuum gives rise to the negative thoughts. Such thoughts during the course of time take the form of fear. This is a real issue.

Entrepreneurship has a lot of uncertainties. This creates a touch of uncertainty in business. But this is quite common and normal for any business unit. Business intelligence is a best way to know about the forthcoming situations.

Not only businesses, almost all works have some type of uncertainty or other. This uncertainty can be handled with the right expertise. Most of the time business founder is well capable of handling. Sometime the right advisory may be taken to sort a particular problem. In all professions the uncertainty factor remains. This factor most of the time give rise to the many opportunities as well. Infact every situation in business offers some opportunity. So, the uncertainty too offers some good prospects.

The business leads to many unknown and unseen destinations. By this I mean the business has immense scope of diversification. Now one business type can change to other business type. Many big corporations started with one product type but moved to other product type during the course of business and its journey. So business travels many unknown and undiscovered paths. But this type of things is the real fun not phobias. But this may at times create a sense of fear to the people who are not in business. This is a real-world situation. But the people who are in business can make the best in such situations.

The flipside of this is the right knowledge and mentorship. These two can be the real solution to almost all phobias related to business. This can be a great learning as well. This is the way of entrepreneurship. With knowledge and mentorship, the business planning can happen. This plan acts as a real guideline for the pathway of the company. This pathway can create a vision of business. This vision can clarify the fear of unknown. With every passing day the experience develops. Experience can lead to a way forward. With the experience that different situations of business can be dealt with easily. This clears the business pathway.

This is further instrumental in fighting the fear of unknown. This phobia is quite uncommon with the people who are not engaged or related with business. The right concept of business and the knowledge of business process are required to tackle this. This is a great way to go ahead with business. Business journey has a lot of ups and downs. This too creates a sense of phobia. This phobia must be fought with right knowledge and mindset.

8. The fear of incurring loss

The profit and loss are the two sides of the business. Business cycle gets both the phases at some point of time or other. The loss creates a sense of phobia amongst many people. Incurring loss can be too tough and disappointing for an entrepreneur. Loss, at times, give tough time to the business owner. But the phase is quite common with all business founders. Incurring loss phase creates a lot of phobias in the mind of many people. This is the way for the creation of fear in mind.

The word "loss" is sort of terrifying factor that it creates an invisible allergy. The business is a risky activity. It contains a certain percentage of risk. At times, people get terrified with this. Loss maybe situational in business. There may be many reasons for that. This might come up due to the improper cash management, due to bad debt, due to damages etc. But this is just a situation like any other situations in business. Such situation are tough to handle. However, in business there are provisions of many precautionary action for prevention of such type of losses. Regular information, regular checks, business intelligence and business analysis can be of great hep to check this. The right business knowledge and the proper analytical skill can help to prevent the loss-making situation. Expertise gets developed with experience. The business, at times, generates various types of insights and data. Right analysis of such data provides a lot of info about business trends. This trend provides the future prediction of business. This, most of the time, gives many forms of business intelligence for forthcoming times. This is a great instrument.

Losses more into the financial figures. So, the financial statement analysis and regular monitoring of various MIS reports can reveal the forthcoming trend in business. So, this situation can be prevented by many means. In business the number analysis can be of great help. If an entrepreneur can analyse the numbers well, many financial adversities can be prevented. Role of finance team can be very important in this. This is a tool to predetermine any forthcoming loss. This can help a company from many other financial exigencies.

The fear of loss can be checked and analysed. Most of the time the fear develop if there is any previous bad experience. Such bad experience can be with oneself or with known persons. So this creates a sense of insecurity leading to the development of phobias. Search for v as at times magnify the probability of any incident. This phobia is more related to subconscious as the past incidents get embedded to this. So knocking off the fear requires a lot of efforts. This can lead to many hurdles as well.

Fear of loss is not something which is uncommon. This is quite common. Right knowledge can be of help to come out of this. This makes many people worried about their next step. Many get into dilemma. Many delays their start. This makes the process doubtful at times. This phobia can even develop from the lack of proper knowledge. People who are not having proper knowledge about business processes, develop such kind of phobias in their mind. This is some of the common phobia this can be compared with the phobia of going to school in children. With the passage of time phobia slowly vanish is.

Like this there could be many other situations which develop such kind of fears and phobias. So, it is important that such kind of circumstances should be properly analysed. Right knowledge guidance and mentorship plays an important role in overcoming such kind of circumstances and related phobias.

Dealing With Phobias

CHAPTER V

How To Face The Challenge

I must say, considering fear or phobia as a challenge can prohibit as becoming a barrier in work. Every challenge can be tackled and likewise every fear can be countered. Always remember that the entrepreneurship is a very systematic and highly scientific activity. There is no scope for any phobia. Right knowledge and right handholding can help to counter this to the fullest.

Challenges will keep coming day in and day out. This will lead to the great journey call entrepreneurship. These challenges need to be well dealt with. Right knowledge and planning are the key over her. So, the right mindset is important. One must fight this out. This makes a great way for the business journey.

Challenges like phobias have to be fought. These with the right fightbacks, backs out. This is not that difficult rather what is required , is the right way out as per the problem faced. This is the real key to face the situation. Here I have mentioned few points which will help a person to deal with the fear of entrepreneurship.

CHAPTER VI

Knowledge

Knowledge is a great weapon. This makes a person armed with so many positive traits. Knowledge creates amazing power inside a person. This is a powerful method of countering phobias & fears.

Why knowledge is important?

Knowledge is a great tool at the sharpest weapon. Knowledge not only helps to fight phobia but also helps in many ways. Knowledge enhances our vision. It creates pathway for the next leap in life. At the same time knowledge helps to gain the various type of vision about the business and entrepreneurship. Knowledge leads to new steps in business.

Knowledge also clarifies many concepts and fundamentals. These concepts and fundamentals of the are the basics. These basics help in start, operation, and growth. So, knowledge is a great starter. It is an investment which gives compounded returns. Every successful person has one habit in common the regularly gain knowledge. Warren buffet was once asked about his secret of success. His answer was "Read 500 pages like this every day. That's how the knowledge works. It builds up like compound interest." This emphasises the importance of knowledge.

Before starting a business one must know about the business streams. Rather a person must do this before even thinking of business. This clarifies all doubts which person can have in mind. This is a great step. One must know about:

i. **Process:** A business is a combination of multiple processes. As a founder of the business one must know all the processes in details. This makes a person confident. At the same time knowing all business processes can help to overcome any types of exigencies. Knowledge of processes also helps to run the business operations smoothly. Knowledge of processes also help to overcome any issues which might come up during the course of operations. This is a boon for business. At the same time people with phobia too can get benefited from this stream of knowledge.

ii. **Practices:** Along with processes one must know the practices of the business. This varies from industry to industry. Before thinking of business, one must know the business practices. Best practices of the trade can be of the great help for any type of business for aspiring entrepreneurs. This is a great learning lesson for everyone. Business practices can also say about the industry and various established processes. Knowing these practices can help to fight phobias to a great extent. One must know about the finance, operations, production, and related practices. These practices can be age old ones and might require modification. But the knowing them can really open the mind.

iii. **Legal and compliances:** Legal work at times might seem like a scary friction for an entrepreneur. But it is not. People get scared due to the lack of knowledge. For the companies to perform one has to abide by the legal framework. In other words, one has to follow the laws of the land. At the same time government authorities of every country setup framework for operating a business. One must follow that as well. This is called compliance. It is an obligation for entrepreneurs to follow these frameworks. At times, entrepreneurs find this bit complicated and fear missing those. One must not get worried on this. At first one must have gain knowledge. After the start of the company, they must allocate a consultant for these matters. If one is not well versed, the role of consultant can be of great help. This help can save a business founder from all legal and compliance related hassles. these hassles can easily be avoided by gaining the right knowledge.

What type of knowledge?

Next question comes as a start-up founder or an aspiring entrepreneur, what type of knowledge one must have? There could be a lot of points for this. But I am taking up 3 points for this

i. **Generic knowledge:** The generic knowledge refers to the general business knowledge. This includes knowledge about business which is applicable to almost all businesses. This includes accounts knowledge, general management, human resources management etc. This knowledge helps to start, run and operate a business. This also involves problem solving and troubleshooting. This is required to get a clear concept about business. The clearer the concept, lesser are the phobias. Phobias originate due to lack of knowledge. Lack of knowledge also creates a lot of misconceptions. Generic knowledge clarifies the concept of business. Every aspiring entrepreneur must have this knowledge.

ii. **Industry specific knowledge:** Every industry requires a specific set of knowledge which is specific to that industry. This helps to understand the practices of the industry. Best practices of the industry, may be learnt before stepping into the industry. This gives a lot of points to learn. Every industry offers a lot to learn. The learning phase requires some form of knowledge which helps to establish the coordination and the best relation amongst the industry peers. This relation can only grow and mature if you are having a right knowledge about the industry in which you are venturing into. Industry knowledge also distinguishes a particular form of work from other industries. This is where the knowledge comes in picture. This also helps in many other ways.

iii. **Knowledge in particular stream or topic:** This knowledge is highly specific. This acts as a super specific steam of knowledge. This is very high skillset. This type of knowledge is required to perform or supervise the specific tasks. These tasks are generally the tasks of high importance. Such task can make or break a business. So, some specific tasks of high importance must be well studied by the people who are aspiring entrepreneurs. This can clarify their thoughts and will make them to be more confident. This can remove any phobia or any type of hurdles. Specific knowledge can make one specialized with a stream of business operations. This type of knowledge is must for troubleshooting. It is obvious that one cannot gain knowledge about all the processes of business. But he or she must have the knowledge about the procedures of business.

Modes of getting knowledge

Today's age is the age of information and the knowledge and the information flows in from all directions. One has to channelize those. In digital world many open channels of knowledge are available. So before one plans to opt for business, the gain of knowledge must be planned. A founder has to ascertain what knowledge to be gained. Once this is ascertained, then the channels or the mode of getting knowledge also can be explored.

I am mentioning here some common channels of knowledge gain.

i. **Books:** Books are the great sources of knowledge. They are the traditional sources and very trusted sources. Regular studies of various business books can clarify a lot of concepts. And it helps in gaining the pure form of knowledge. More the concepts get clear, the phobias start vanishing. The clarity of vision will also happen. This also makes the mind uncluttered.

ii. **YouTube**: YouTube is a great platform for learning. Almost all types of topics have their content in YouTube. So, if you search any form of content you are sure to get a lot of results.

iii. **Podcasts**: Podcast is a great mode to listen to influencers, authors and many successful people. You may get a lot of knowledge about the business from this. Not only knowledge you may also get a lot of new and upcoming concepts.

iv. **User based contacts**. Internet offers a lot of user-based contacts, where many users share their knowledge. These acts as a powerhouse of knowledge. However, at times the little refinement of knowledge may be required. Blogs are one of the greatest sources of knowledge. Many sites put user generated content as well.

v. **Social media:** social media are very powerful platform. Best part is, such platforms are interactive. This allows two-way communications. Apart from being interactive they are many learning options as well. Many users share articles, videos, information, photos etc. Many do live sessions on various subjects. So, if you follow right person or page, you are sure to get a lot of informative stuff. There are many audio platforms as well. Example can be Clubhouse, Facebook audio rooms etc. Every social media offers a lot of features for likeminded people wherein they can share their views and interact.

vi. **Newsletters and magazines:** These are the sources of knowledge which goes on periodic basis. You may subscribe to specific industry magazines. This gives a lot of insight on various subjects. Newsletters are available with almost all websites. You may get your email subscribed, for receiving email newsletters. Even influencers too have their newsletter options. These offer insights and knowledge on various upcoming topics and subjects.

vii. **Associations:** There are many influential associations across the globe - some operate at a regional level and some operate at global level. These associations offer a lot of knowledge sharing sessions on various topics. Some of the topics can be even new and upcoming one. These are the great sources of sharing knowledge. Most of the time the sessions are interactive. This also helps in doubt clearance.

viii. **Peer to peer knowledge sharing:** This is a great way to share and gain knowledge. Peer can act as a great source of knowledge. Many times, peer give a lot of productive and practical knowledge. This is easy and the best way to get the first-hand knowledge. Many times, peer give the way for uncommon type of knowledge. Many doubts clearance chances too come up. Discussions are productive in most of the cases.

Like this, there are so many ways of gaining knowledge. Knowledge helps to clarify the concept. With clear concept, things go clear, and the phobias fade away. Knowledge is always a boon for anything. It is always recommended to gain related knowledge before starting any project. This makes one's mind uncluttered. This is the key for any foundation step.

CHAPTER VII

Mentorship

Mentorship is a blessing in business. This gives direction to the business. Mentors are the experienced persons in business. They have loads of experience which they share with aspiring entrepreneurs. This is a great experience. Mentorship also acts as a process of hand-holding a new entrepreneur. Mentorship helps an aspiring entrepreneur to overcome initial hiccups. This also acts as a guide to most of the situations which a person faces. This gives a confidence to entrepreneurs and with this the phobias fade away. This is a process which acts as a guiding lamp.

This process at times is difficult to get. Most of the time right mentors are not available to all start-up founders. Membership can help you to select the right path for your business.

The concept of mentorship

Mentorship refers to the relation between the person who offers his knowledge experience and guidance to the person who is seeking it. Mentor is referred as someone who offers his or her wisdom knowledge and advice to someone with less experience. Mentee is referred as a person who seek the guidance for the next step. Mentee receives significant benefits from successful mentorship. The process of mentoring is similar to coaching. But unlike coaching mentors most of the time do not go for direct monetary transactions. One may go for informal mentorship sessions with known people. At some point of time, one may choose to take up formal mentorship session by various industrial associations and various business bodies. Many a times government of various places also arrange for mentorship programs.

Mentorship happens at various stages. This may be for a start of business, running of business or even during the scale up phase. This is unlike consultancy or advisory processes. These processes are totally different.

In mentorship, mentee gets benefited from the guidance of mentor. This process goes on for long term basis. With every passing day mentee gets benefits from mentor. This effort is ongoing process. The flow of knowledge is a great source of learning. Many successful entrepreneurs have benefited from the concept. During an interview with CNBC, Bill Gates credit Warren Buffet. for teaching him how to deal with tough situations.

Richard Branson requested for mentorship from Sir Freddie Laker, the British airline entrepreneur while Virgin Atlantic was struggling. Mark Zuckerberg credited his success to Steve Jobs. There are many such examples in the world.

The reasons you need a mentor.

Almost every entrepreneur needs a mentor. Mentors can be the game changers for all. The wisdom shared by mentor are off immense help to them. Getting a mentor is quite different from hiring a consultant.

(i)Gaining knowledge beyond book: Mentors are very knowledgeable and very experienced people from the industry. They have loads of experiences. This experience turns to knowledge. This knowledge mixed with experience acts as a gold mine for entrepreneur. This is of great significance. Right knowledge is a blessing. It is an experience with best teacher. This teacher teachers some of the finest lessons in life. However, an aspiring entrepreneur or one who is new to start-ups are devoid of experience. So, here you want someone by your site to guide.

(ii) Guide for success and overcoming hurdles: Successful entrepreneurs mostly have mentors. Mentors hold their hand and take them through the journey of entrepreneurship. This journey is very tough and has lot of ups and downs. Many times, an entrepreneur get stuck or fail to decide on a certain situation. Mentor, here, acts as a God under such situations. This type of situations is quite common and frequent in business. If you get right mentors, the chance of success increases manifold. Mentor provides industry connections, right advice, moral and ethical guidance.

(iii) Networking and growth connections: Mentors are the industry leaders. They come with huge business network. They introduce a mentee to his or her own network of business connections. This will be of great benefit for the mentee in long and short run. Mentor can introduce you to network of clients', investors, consultants, authorities, government agencies etc. These connections are of immense help to them mentee. This can be a great opportunity to the start-up founder otherwise building such connection could have taken years

(iv) Increase emotional quotient: Business involves taking decisions every now and then. Right decisions are good for business and vice versa. In case of entrepreneur being new in business, the chance of taking a wrong decision is bit high. Also, business brings many emotional moments and many heated moments as well. Such moments make business bit vulnerable. Under such circumstances, it is important to be emotionally stable. Having a mentor helps an entrepreneur to be emotionally stable with proper and right guidance. It also leads to proper emotional quotient.

(v) Hand on encouragement: Businesses is full of ups and downs. Down phases are really tough and depressing. People who are not in business will not understand this. A mentor being experienced in this field, can hold your hands in such situations. Mentor will encourage you to face and overcome the situation. This encouragement is really required by entrepreneur at some point of the journey. Encouragement, at times, becomes much needed stiff for a start-up founder.

(vi) Helps to answer questions and clarify concepts: An entrepreneur has a lot to question on business concepts, processes and operation. Even on problems and hurdles. At times, an entrepreneur finds it difficult to get the personalised answers. Generic answers are available all across the spaces, but an entrepreneur required personalised answers. This is because a sample problem faced by two entrepreneurs may be due to different reasons. Their solution you can be different. So, entrepreneur have to get personalised solution for their problems. Many a times a start-up founder might not have a clear concept of the business. Here, also the relevance of concept varies from person to person. One concept might be relevant in a specific way to one entrepreneur. However for the other entrepreneur it might be relevant in different way.

(vii) Scope of general improvement: Mentors are unlike consultants. They help all round development of an entrepreneurs. This is the real benefit of mentorship. Mentors develop a personal bond with mentees. This results in identification of many weaknesses. Once the weaknesses are identified, one can work to overcome those. This helps to develop the overall personality of a person.

(viii) Help in strategy making: As I have mentioned, mentors are highly experienced people in business world. They can help in formulating the business strategies for your business. Strategy plays an important role in business. In fact this is indispensable part of business. Right strategy helps to grow the business. As a new entrepreneur, you might not be able to pinpoint the factors required for strategy making. A guidance from an experienced mentor acts as a boon for you.

3As of Mentorship

One of the very common concepts in mentorship is "3A's of mentorship". Now these 3As make the foundation of the mentorship journey. These 3As are said to be one of the finest pillars for this journey.

Mentorship is more offer relation. This relation helps to overcome most of the business hurdles. The mentorship foundation relies on 3A's.

(i) Active listening. A mentor in most of the cases is an active listener. He listens to the mentees. He listens to his or her problems, issues, confusion, and fears. He is important listener to mentee's problem. Now this gives mentee a psychological boost. Many finds a place where he can let a person hear to his problems. This situation is a great boost for an entrepreneur. This stage leads to the proper understanding of the problem of entrepreneur. In this case mentor lends his ears first and then provides the solution to his or her problems.

(ii) Availability: Mentor has to be always available for a mentee. This provides a moral support for the start-up founder. Physical availability may not be required for certain situations. But always remember mentors time is also important. He has to plan his time properly. Ask for physical availability only when it is extremely required or absolutely necessary. Nowadays mentor can even be consulted online. Online meets can be of great help. Regular physical or online meet with mentee is quite important. Next concept is emotional availability. This is the virtual concept. Many situations requires emotional support by mentor. Emotional availability of mentor is required in many situations of business. Many of the time mentors are available out of business hours. This is a great blessing for the start-up founders.

(iii) Analysis: With every problem or situation which start-up founder faces a mentor need to analyse it. It must be done properly followed by the suggestion of solution. This analysis is done by mentor as they are the people with lots of experiences. With their knowledge and experience a mentor can read a situation and give feedback. This is quite important for an entrepreneur. This also results in getting solutions. Analytical techniques of a mentor can act as a boon for an entrepreneur.

4 stages of mentorship.

Mentorship is a long term journey. This journey has various stages. This can be broadly classified into 4 stages.

(i) Initiation: This is the first stage of mentorship. This step starts the relationship of mentor and mentee. They know each other in this phase. They formally discuss their common in interest like values, future, goals and dreams. This step acts as an orientation phase for mentor and mentee. This stage is quite important as both mentor and mentee should discuss and clarify their expectations. This phase can be bit different at times.

There can be confusions, difficulty in communication or even a gap of communication. Development of trust develops only when; this stage is taken up properly. Comfort and trust development is quite important to carry on with the journey. So, both mentor and mentee have to come up with clear expectation from each other.

(ii) Scope of collaboration and goal setting: Once the orientation phase of mentorship is done and both mentor and mentee know each other properly, then the next comes the stage. In this phase, the scope of collaboration and goal setting happens. They agree on initial expectations and define the goal which need to be achieved. This is a stage of defining the strategies to achieve the goal. The action plan for the journey is planned in this stage. The next step of journey is planned here. This includes the way to take up the relationship, establishing the rules & boundaries of mentorship journey and to create shared responsibilities. There are many other vital points and not easy to talk about. But mentor and mentee must know and plan these vital points before the start of the mentorship journey. This may be the right time to come up and modify the full plan of mentorship. This helps to reap the benefits of the journey. This also helps to prevent any future disputes.

(iii) Growth: Once the goal setting stages is done. The mentoring journey enters the phase three. This is the phrase when the mentor and mentee start working towards the goal which is set in the stage number two. From here, the learning graph goes up mentor can lead the journey and open the opportunities for mentee. This is the real working phase. They share knowledge and experience. Here, the feedback too flows in. Flow of honest and constructive feedback is the need of the hour. Feedback helps a mentee to remain on path and prevent any deviation or errors. This also helps to identify the weaknesses and aids in overcoming those. Regular review and monitoring of the journey is essential. This also helps in achieving the goal.

(iv) Closure: This is the stage when the mentor and mentee formally close their relationship. The reason for this can be end of the journey of achievement of the goal. This not just saying goodbye. This is the stage of thanking each other for the association. Both mentor and mentee harvest their learning experience for future endeavours. A positive closure is recommended for this

Do's And Don'ts of Mentorship !

The journey of mentorship is very sacred journey. So, the right etiquettes for the journey is important. Both mentor and mentee have to follow certain points.

Presenting the following do's for mentorship

i. Have respect towards the mentor
ii. Present and clarify your expectations before start
iii. Dedicate adequate time towards mentorship process
iv. Openly discuss about goals, strategies and path to achieve at the frame of time
v. Raise your performance bar
vi. Plan regular review sessions
vii. Respect mentors time
viii. Communicate failures and shortcomings
ix. Communicate your fears and challenges
x. Discuss and work out a backup plan for business
xi. Discuss chances of failures and the ways to hold back or prevent it
xii. Discuss and make step by step plan for goal achieving
xiii. Discuss the probable hurdles of the plan and ways to face them
xiv. Discuss modes of communication as mentors may be busy with their own business as well
xv. Make a log of sessions for future learning purpose and reference

Presenting don'ts of mentorship

i. Do not take criticism and negative feedbacks personally
ii. Do not skip steps of mentorship
iii. Do not get upset if the results take time to appear
iv. Do not take journey as guarantee for success
v. Do not complaint
vi. Do not only count the monetary benefits
vii. Do not crib and cry with setbacks
viii. Do not shy to ask questions
ix. Do not shy to discuss strategies
x. Do not hide your mistakes
xi. Do not take away the trust due to initial setbacks
xii. Do not burn the bridge of relation after closure
xiii. Do not leave professional behaviour during the mentorship journey

xiv. Do not shy to communicate your doubts and fears

xv. Do not take mentor or mentorship process for granted

The techniques of mentorship

Process of mentorship is a voluntary service. So, the right way of mentorship is important. This depends on the mentor and mentee requirements. Certain ways of these are suitable for someone and some are suitable for others. Below are the techniques which are most frequently used.

(i) The group mentorship technique: In this type of technique, mentor provides mentorship to a group of people. This helps a group of similar type of aspirants or start-up founders. The group of people with the similar goals suit this kind of mentorship technique. This is suitable for schools or colleges. Most of the time generic start-ups topics are touched in this type of mentorship. The personalised care might not be possible in this. However using this technique, a lot of person can reap the benefits of mentorship

(ii) Peer mentorship technique: In this type of mentorship technique, peer addresses an individual or a group by sharing experience. The experience of peer helps them in a lot of ways. It helps mentees to overcome initial hurdles of business starting. This also helps in clearing objections and dealing with phobias.

(iii) One on one mentorship technique: In this type of technique only mentor and mentee are involved. This type of mentorship is preferred by most of the people. The advantage of this type of technique is that, a mentee can get attention in full. Most of the time mentee and their problem are not similar to others. So, one on one mentorship can be best suited for this.

(iv) Distant or virtual mentorship: This technique became common going to the COVID19 pandemic. This makes access of mentor easy. Mentor and mentee can discuss the matter sitting hundreds of miles away. This also saves the travelling time of mentor. In other words, mentor can do the sessions with many mentees together. This even allows flexibility of time.

Types of mentoring.

To classify the concept of mentoring, this can further classified as

Based on type of interactions

Mentor and mentee interaction happens in many ways. This type of interaction helps to understand that type of mentoring.

(i) Formal mentoring: In this type of mentoring mentor and mentee formally get into the journey. Proper plans are chalked out and proper frameworks are planned. Every part of interaction takes the formal mode.

(ii) Informal mentorship: This generally happens in the known circle of people. This is the informal way of mentor-mentee relationship. In this type of the formal way of mentorship journey do not happen. Many times, interactions happen for specific issues only. Also, the goal setting may or may not take place in this type of mentorship journey.

Based on number of mentors and mentees.

Number of mentors and mentees too lead to the classification of mentorship process.

(i) Group mentoring: In this type of mentoring one person, mentors a group of mentees. Mentees interact with mentor for their mentorship journey. The benefit of this method is a lot of people can get the benefit of mentorship at a time. Disadvantages personal attention cannot be given.

(ii) Team mentoring: In this type of mentoring, a group of mentors interact with the number of mentees. This has an added advantage over the group mentoring technique. The mentees get benefited from many mentors. Some mentors are expert in certain subject and some our expert in other subjects and aspects of business. So, the knowledge quantum goes high as compared to group mentoring.

Based on identity of mentees

Mentees come up from various backgrounds. So, mentoring all might require a bit different approach. So, the type of mentorship is also classified based on that.

(i) Identity segregated mentoring: Mentis comes from various backgrounds. Their preferences may be different. So, in this type of mentorship the mentees who come from similar background are paired together for mentorship sessions. This helps to address the problems of similar nature and of similar types.

(iii) Hybrid mentoring: In this type of mentoring mentees of various backgrounds are mentored together. Benefit of this is, mingling with the various background enhances the knowledge and skillset of all.

Each type of mentoring has its own advantages and disadvantages. Mentor and mentee have to pick and choose the best suitable method.

5 rules of effective mentorship

Mentoring journey has to be right. This is a sacred journey. Under all circumstances, the sanctity of this journey has to be preserved. It is important that the journey of mentorship should be properly defined. Right mentor and mentee match must be done, and it should be done in a well-defined manner.

I am mentioning here 5 rules which can help in effective mentorship.

(i) Effective communication: The communication plays an important role in mentorship journey. The communication is the first rule of this. The right flow of communication must be established between them. Mentee should clearly communicate his or her doubts, fears, confusions, expectations and purpose. The purpose of seeking mentorship is going to be the best thing to do as an aspiring start-up founder. It is important to communicate the expectations. One must communicate the fears as well. Request the mentor to help in respect with various spheres of business you need help. Communicate those clearly.

(ii) Be engaging and collaborative: Mentorship journey has to be engaging. Both mentor and mentee must engage in this. It is not one-sided journey. The engagement must be proper. Engagement gives proper direction. This leads to collaboration as well. Collaboration is one of the key outcomes of mentorship. Collaborations are the boon for any kind of business or start up journey. Engagement with mentor and the guided collaboration can wipe-out the fear factors from the minds of start-up founders.

(iii) Sail a tight ship: Mentor's guidance often comes manifold. So, it is important for mentor and mentee to know each other's expectations. This is the key pointer before start of journey. The expectations then must take the form of goals. This need to be subdivided into long term and short-term goals.

After understanding the expectations' goal determination has to be done. The goal workout must be done properly. This might be a time taking affair. Once the goals are finalised, it has to be classified into long term and short term once. When this exercises is done, then the mentor and mentee need to work the pathway for that. The short-term goals can be achieved quickly. Whereas the long-term goals are achieved over a period of time. What is important is to have the right direction and method-based planning. This is what the mentorship aims for. Regular review of processes is must for this journey. So, the sale of the ship of mentorship should be rightly planned. There is no scope for any divided attention.

(iv) Define the phases properly: I have already described the mentorship as a journey. In order to walk through the journey, the journey need to be well defined. This is the real key. The journey can be classified into 8 pieces. I am noting here those.

I. **Seeking phase:** This is the face where the aspiring entrepreneur or the start-up founder notes his or her problems and seeks mentorship. This is basically the search phase. The mentor and mentee search for a right connect. Before the search, defining the purpose and the problem is important. These are two terms, which are well noted here. In fact, this is a pre mentoring phase.

II. **Introduction phase:** This is the phase where in the mentor and mentee gets introduced to each other. They start knowing each other and shared their expectations. This phase must be done properly and with utmost care.

III. **The work out phase:** Once the intro part phase is over, one must go for workout phase. In this phase goal is sort and plans are chalked out. This is followed by defining the pathway. This is the start of execution phase.

IV. **The journey phase:** Once the goals are defined and plans are chalked out the journey of mentorship starts. This leads to the share of experience and guidance. Mentee gets benefit from mentor's experience.

V. **Review phase:** Once the journey starts the review of progress happens. The review also overcome all type of doubts, hurdles and objections. This also checks any type of deviations. This may call for revision of the way.

VI. **Completion face:** This is the face where, goal defined, before the start of the mentorship journey, gets accomplished. This is the phase of achievement.

VII. **Reconciliation phase:** In this phase after completion, the mentor and mentee, decide whether to call off the journey or to start afresh. This is the basically a discussion phase.

VIII. **Transition phase:** In this phase mentor and mentee decides to call off the collaboration. This phase comes to play once the goal is accomplished. This is a thanks giving phase.

All these 8 phases should be defined properly this makes the journey proper and well defined.

Follow the "CHAMP" way

Champ is the effective method for mentorship. This consists of five easy steps:

I. **Credibility:** In the journey of mentorship, the credibility of mentor and mentee matters. This acts as a base for the journey. One must take care of this factor. The question on credibility spoils the journey.

II. **Honesty:** One must remain honest during the entire journey. This is an important aspect. Honesty keeps the journey sacred to the core. This makes the mentor and mentee more and engrossed in the journey.

III. **Attentiveness:** Attentiveness of mentee helps him or her to take the full advantage of the journey. This makes the journey efficient.

IV. **Maintaining relation:** Maintaining the good and professional relationship is important. This makes the journey long lasting. Mentor or mentee relation is a sacred relation.

V. **Positivity:** Positivity is an important factor in life. Business journey is full of ups and downs. At times, it makes a person depressing. So, the touch of positivity is important in this journey. This makes the journey interesting.

Not prone to failure.

Mentorship is a guiding journey. It is not a magic wand. It does not provide any immunity to failure. It is a process of hand holding an aspiring an entrepreneur or a start-up founder. One must know and understand that failures are one of the indispensable factors in mentorship journey. Every entrepreneur in this world has faced failures at some point of time or other.

Mentorship is a pious journey. It does not guarantee success. One must understand that success and failures are the two sides of the same coin. These two phases arrive over at different time in journey. So always remember, mentorship is a guidance not a guarantee. This is a blessing in the journey of entrepreneurship.

CHAPTER VIII

Incubation

This is a new process in many parts of the globe. The business incubation is a process in which a start-up company gets initial support with full scale range of services for starting and related matters. The institution which gives such type of services are called incubators. Start-up companies get an array of services which involves arranging office space, company support, mentorship, guidance etc. The business incubation process is at times sponsored by private companies, corporate bodies, or Government. Most of the services provided by incubators are either free or below market rates.

Apart from offering multiple services incubators offers opportunities for mentoring, networking, and legal consultancy. Many times, government provides a lot of additional benefit to these as well. Starting a business in isolation is scary, at times. Incubation centres offers an ecosystem for business. This takes away initial hurdles and fears. This makes an aspiring start-up confident about the journey.

An overview and history

Business incubation is defined as a system or environment made to accelerate the growth and development of a start-up company through an array of business support services. This may include physical space, coaching, mentorship, capital, common services, networking, legal assistance and market support. The companies or organisations which provides such services are called business incubators.

The origin of this concept is traced in 1959. A person named Joseph L Mancuso, in the USA opened Batavia Industrial Center in Batavia, New York. That was a warehouse. In USA, this concept took full-fledged shape in 1980s. This concept traveled to Europe in various ways. In 1980s there are only 12 business incubators in North America. This number touch 1400 in October 2006. Her majesty's treasury identified around 25 incubators in United Kingdom in the year 1997. By 2005 UKBI identified around 270 incubators. In 2005, North American incubator program assisted more than 27,000 companies that provide employment to over 100,000 workers and generated revenue of 17 billion U.S. dollars. Incubation concept went well with the developing countries as well. Many Governments of various countries too supported the concept of business incubation. This is worth to mention that the first incubation centre in Silicon Valley was Catalyst Technologies. It was founded by American businessman Nolan Kay Bushnell, The founder of Atari. He was named one of the "Newsweek's 50 Men Who Changed America".

Importance of business incubators

Business incubation is a great blessing for start-ups. These incubators offer a complete ecosystem to business units. This is a great opportunity for initial stage of business journey.

a. **Provides an ecosystem:** Incubation of businesses is like a full ecosystem. Such incubators provide a lot of facilities to start-ups. This may include office space, common services etc. This is a boon for new companies.

b. **Common space for interactions:** Such facilities offer a place or a platform to interact amongst themselves. This makes a platform to discuss their problems and business prospects.

c. **Creates a start-up culture:** Start up journey is quite lonely. This helps bringing many start-ups under one roof. This makes a culture of start-up.

d. **Encourages taking up entrepreneurship:** This provides an encouragement for start-up and entrepreneurship. This helps in many ways to overall business environment of the place.

e. **Benefit of government schemes:** The government of various places runs many such schemes. Generally, the benefit of various Government schemes is distributed through various institutions. Incubators are the front runner for those.

f. **Selection of good ideas:** Incubators are run by experience people. These people pick up bright business ideas and its potential. Such are nurtured and refined at incubation centres. This becomes the best for bigger business of future.

g. **Operate at ground level:** Operators of business incubation centres are well versed with local areas. This helps to locate the bright business ideas at the ground level.

h. **Connect and support for local government:** These incubators, at times, act as a start-up support system for local government bodies. Government approaches them for various solutions for existing problems.

a. **Potential employment generation:** Business incubators have potential for becoming big time employment generator in future. So, this stage is the initial phase of a bigger journey.

j. **Helps in micro-businesses:** In rural areas, micro businesses are plenty. These micro businesses have huge potentials. Incubators can pick up and choose those and nurture them to become well organized businesses.

k. **Throwing competitions:** Many times, Government agencies or corporate bodies invites business unit for various challenges. This creates a healthy competitive environment for innovation in the country.

How it works

Business incubation is like full time environment. One has to go through right processors to get into the system. Business units looking for incubation has to go through various processes to qualify for this.

a. **Selection process:** Incubators look for start-ups which are looking for incubation. These start-ups maybe from a specific industry or from various different industries. These are selected through either a competitive process or handpicked based on certain qualities. At times, corporate bodies, chambers too put their recommendations. Generally, these selections are done by a board. After the process is done selected start-ups are informed formally. Most of the time viability of start-up idea are considered. Overall start-up system of the company are also scrutinised.

b. **Entry to incubation:** Once the selection process of incubation is done and the formal contract between the incubator and start-up is executed. Start-up gets an entry to the incubation. Start-up gets access to all facilities of the incubation centre. Most of the time environment includes likeminded people. These people are the source of networking. Space is also allocated to the start-up for their functioning. They get there for a period of few months to few years. Slowly phobias and doubt fade away.

c. **Start of operations and guidance:** This is the phase when start-up start their operation, while in incubation. The company get a lot of facilities and benefits. They get guidance is as well. This helps to make a lively environment for start-ups. Once the guidance and the positive environment effects come up, the clarity gets lit up in the mind of start-up founders.

d. **The flourishing phase:** With likeminded environment and able guidance start-up founders starts flourishing. The face initial hotels in an organised way. Once the initial hurdles are faced and sorted start-up operations becomes quite organised and a regulate This leads to flourishing phase of the start-up. This phase is characterised by generation of revenue. Start-up founder start seeing ROI in this phase.

e. **The exit phase:** This is the phase when a start-up founder decides to exit the incubation facilities. Many times, incubation has a time fram Once the time frame gets over start-up has to move. It creates a vacancy for new start-ups. The cycle goes on. The incubation gives support to a start-up in crucial years of business. Once the business gets established the facilities of incubation may be withdrawn. Exit phase is a goodbye phase, with the new beginning for start-up.

Types of incubators

Incubators are classified based on the various factors. These are at times are classified based on industries, based on setup, based on functions etc but the function of all are more or less same.

Incubators can be classified into below categories

i. **Corporate incubators:** These are run by the corporate bodies. They facilitate the creation of start-up environment. Most of the time this acts as a part of their CSR initiative. These types of incubators, help start-up to use their own facilities and resources. Their team even extends mentoring help as well. This gives start-up and exposure to the corporate environment. They get a touch of corporate culture, corporate ethics and corporate systems. This help start-ups to get acquainted with the corporate systems. All these are helpful in long run.

ii. **Academic incubators:** These types of incubators remain attached to the educational institutions. These types of incubators deal with the projects related to academics. Generally, these incubators joining process has a pre-requisite of being a student. They provide a lot of opportunity to test the various concepts or ideas. One can also learn a lot of start-up related concepts over here. Many times, they provide assistance to raise seed funding. Motive of this is to engrave the idea of entrepreneurship and clarify the concept.

iii. **Social incubators:** These types of incubators host the companies which make a social impact. In other words, they host start-ups which solves a social problem or provides any solution to any long-lasting society related issue.

iv. **Local economic development incubator:** This type of incubators provide support to the local level business. This might include craft or service business. They work for local and small businesses. They are main moto is to provide the support to the business of local area for the economic development. Many a times, small and unorganised businesses get help from these types of incubators. The unorganised business forms the base of business in rural and suburban areas. Most of the time they are most neglected business segments. These type of incubators or boon for the rural sector.

There is another way of classifying incubators. These are based on the type of incubation facilities - physical or virtual. Let's know these in detail. This classification took a leap during COVID19 pandemic.

i. **Physical incubators:** This is a traditional approach. In this type of incubators start-up has to get into incubation centre physically. This helps them to access the incubation facilities available at that centre. Company physically starts working from the centre. This approach makes a company use its address for operations.

ii. **Virtual incubator:** This type of incubation allows start-ups to operate from a remote location without being in the incubation centre physically. This is a new concept and uses technology to connect with start-ups. Here, the start-ups are guided and counselled using the virtual technologies. In fact, this is a revolutionary concept.

Incubators are also classified based on industries. Many types of incubators incubate start-ups of a specific industry. This specializes on that specific industry type. So, the industry specific classification of incubators not uncommon. I am mentioning here some specific industry type incubation centres.

i. **Kitchen incubators:** As the name suggests this type of incubators provide support to food related start-ups. This industry is growing fast. Many people with passion for culinary art are comes here. It is good to have industry specific start-up. The real benefit of these types of incubators is that they take start-ups of the same industry. Most of the time start-ups of the same industry faces similar issues or same kind of challenges. So, it becomes easy to address those. This type of incubators at times offers kitchen space also. Mentoring and other benefits are always there.

ii. **Medical incubators:** There are so many healthcare start-ups in the world. These types of start-ups are growing at a rapid pace. Medical incubators facilitate the incubation of healthcare start-ups. Just type includes start-ups dealing with medicines, medical equipment, medical technologies, medical consumables etc. This is a growing industry as healthcare is getting into an innovative environment every passing day. Many times, such start-ups require a lot of paperwork to start operations. Incubators extend a helping hand for this.

iii. **Technology incubators:** The technology start-ups form a major part of the start-up community in the world. They require some special type of incubation setup to deal with their regular problems. So, the technology incubators put that technology start-ups into incubation. This type of incubation, at times, also provides with research and development facilities. As on date, majority of incubators are the technology incubators.

Like this there are many ways based on which incubators are classified.
Application for incubation.
Incubation at time seems like a competition. This is required to pick and select the able start-up company. This helps to select the most eligible start-up for the incubation process. In order to do this, every incubation set up an application process. The application process helps an incubator in selection.

Process of selection differs from incubator to incubator. Some of the ways of mentioning here.

I. **Competition:** Many times, competition is put for the selection of start-up. Start-up participates in the competition. This could be informed of challenges or problems solving way. Start-ups are selected from this.

II. **Pitching:** Many times start-ups are asked to pitch the concept of their business. Based on the pitch and followed by question-and-answer, selection takes place.

III. **Collaboration with organization:** Incubators collaborate with various organisations like government departments, Chamber of Commerce etc. Start-up selection at times happen with collaboration with these organisations.

IV. **Business model submission:** Application is called for submission of business model. After submission, these models are scrutinised by a panel. Decision of panel is taken as guideline for selection of start-ups for incubation.

Like this, there are many other forms of incubation selection. These processes very critical. Selection criteria varies from each other. So, incubation application process is well advertised. These advertisement helps in selection process. Application at times is quite tough. Or proper business plan with all details is indispensable before applying for incubation.

Advantages of incubation

Incubation offers a lot of facilities for start-up founders. This can be a blessing for the new companies. I am mentioning some of the advantages.

I. **Mentorship:** Incubation offers a lot of scope for mentorship. Mentorship is a boon for business. This has a lot of benefits. This acts as a hand holding for new businesses. This is one of the key advantages a new entrant may get. Mentorship helps to overcome many hurdles. It further extends help to strategies the business. A good guidance is what matters.

II. **Advisory:** Starting a proper company might seem like a complicated procedure. This requires right advisory. Advisory is required during start as well as during the functioning of the company. The compliance advisory is also required to avoid compliance failure and penalties. Advisory is another key benefit, incubators offer.

III. **Low-cost utilities:** A company office requires utility. At time utilities are termed as hidden cost. Incubation centre offers utility to the start-ups at a very low cost. This can be in form of office rent, electricity, administrative services etc. This is another great advantage. It saves a lot of expenses for a new company.

IV. **Networking:** Incubation centres offer a lot of opportunities for networking. At times, they also conduct networking sessions. Initial networking can be a great help for a start-up. It helps a new company explore newer avenues of business. This can be a positive impact in due course of time.

V. **Access to resources:** Incubators give access to start-ups. its resources. Resource could be of various types. It could be in form of space, administrative support, equipment etc. At times many incubators provide raw materials for production units too. They even provide support for sale and marketing. Adequate resource support help start-ups to grow and operate properly. Incubators even arrange regular workshops on various subjects as well.

VI. **Access to funding:** One of the major benefits of incubation process is that start-up gets access to fund raising option. Funding is a great requirement of any business. Many great ideas die down due to lack of funding. Incubators use to have a great network for the fundraising process. Many times, government schemes disperse funds for grants through incubators. This gives a start-up founder added advantage. Incubators generally have attached investors. They can help a start-up founder to get access to seed funding in initial stages. One may even check the network of angel investor, which an incubator has. Incubators have specific areas of focus for funding and investment. This helps to bring together a group of investors for business. At times these activities are industry specific.

VII. **Keeping razor-sharp focus:** Incubators can provide much needed structure and environment that helps a start-up founder to have their focus intact on business. In an incubation centre, business setup its already in place. Here, start-up founder does not have to worry about the office utilities and setups. This will help to keep the focus only on the business. This will save the time and helps to focus on business goals and objectives. This helps a company to get stable and keep afloat during the initial years of business.

VIII. **Help in growth:** Guidance, advice, mentorship, and resources helps a company to grow and get stable. This is a real boon. This minimizes is the time taken to go for the next leap. This fastens the growth phase of start-up.

IX. **Facilitates collaboration:** An incubator provides a lot of networking opportunities to a start-up. This leads to much needed collaboration. Collaboration is a great thing. This increases business and helps to get the business rolling. Collaboration also initiates referrals. This aids in increase in business activities and leads to growth.

Disadvantages of incubation

With so many advantages in this. There are few disadvantages as well. Start-up must be well aware of these as well.

I. **Acting as a business unit:** Incubation centres too act as a business unit. This at times go for profit making. Profit, at times, dampens the spirit and the real purpose of entrepreneurship. The profit making, at times, make the facilities sub-standard. This degrades the real purpose of incubation.

II. **Move with trend:** Incubators generally select start-ups which are high on trend. That means the start-up with the current trend or flamboyant trend will get selected. In other words, many start-ups without on trends gets rejected

III. **Application process:** Application process for start-up selection is quite rigorous. Many a times start-up find it tough to get through the process. This is the real hurdle for start-up. Especially start-ups in the rural areas face this hurdle. At times, the application process is too specific for industry concern. Too much competitive environment makes many start-ups devoid of this facility.

IV. **Equity makeover:** Many times, incubators demand an equity share in lieu of the facilities provided. This equity makeover is not liked by many start-up founders. This issue needs to be clarified beforehand.

V. **Interference in day-to-day operations:** Interference in day to day operation of a startup is also a disadvantage. This is rare, but this does happens

The disadvantages of incubation system are quite low as compared to the advantages. Incubation in the right way can be a great step in start-up journey.

Example of business incubators

There are a lot of business incubators across the globe. Nowadays even Tier 2 and tier 3 cities too are getting incubation facilities. Some of the famous business incubators across the world are

i. **Y combinator:** This was founded by Paul Graham in 2005. It is in Palo Alto Silicon Valley. It is run by a team of people and take a lot of applications online. It is referred as one of the oldest start-up incubators. It incubated Dropbox, Airbnb, Instacart, Stripe, Twitch, Reddit just to name a few. Every year they fund a group of new start-ups.

ii. **Ignite:** It is one of the noted names in UK and Europe. It is backed by European Union and collaborated with Google. They have funded more than 150 Start-up companies. It started in the year 2011. There is a lot of pre-accelerators and accelerator programs.

iii. **Melbourne accelerator program:** It is one of the noted name in Australia. It is supported by university of Melbourne and founded in the year 2012. They have tied up with Universal Music Group. They also provide funding assistance to start-ups.

iv. **Startup Rejkjavik:** There are a lot of start-up guidance program. Founded in the year 2012 they offer investment and provide working space. They have wonderful network. That includes inventors, business experts etc.

v. **Chinaccelerator:** It is Shanghai based facility founded in the year 2010. This is a mentorship driven facility. They also invested in start-ups outside China as well. There are members of various funding schemes.

vi. **Startup yard:** It is a Prague based facility. They mostly take up tech start-ups. They have a good access to the companies, corporates and investors. They provide a lot of support during seed funding stage. A noted name in the start-up from this facility is Teskalab.

vii. **Axel Springer Plug & Play Accelerator:** It is located in Berlin. It is founded in the year 2013. It is a joint venture between Axel Springer SE (Noted name in German printing.) They take up startups and even house artists.

viii. **Metavallon:** It is established in the year 2011. They incubate tech start-ups. They even developed Metavallon VC. They provide mentorship, guidance, coaching, networking, talent acquisition and funding opportunities.

ix. **Startup boot camp:** It is founded in the year 2010. They facilitate the incubation for tech and food tech start-up. They have program across the globe like in Singapore, London, Mumbai, Delhi, Amsterdam to name a few. They help early stage start-up founders to scale their business. They have partnered with investors, mentors, business founders etc

x. **Highline Beta:** This was founded in the year 2014. They offer initial support and extend marketing related support also. Noted start-up originating from this is META - later acquired by Chan Zuckerberg initiative and Fambit acquired by Google. This is best in Toronto

Accelerators

This is another concept in business. This is similar to the concept of incubation. It helps a business to give a headstart. They accelerate the processes of business. They help a business or a startup to hit the market andmake prototype.Accelerator emphasizes on rapid growth of startup.

This concept is more suitable for start-up companies who want to reduce their time to get into the market and grow at a rapid pace.

The function of incubator and accelerators are almost the same but with a little bit of difference. Incubators assist a start-up company from an idea stage. They help to work and refine the idea and help to build from scratch. On the other hand an accelerator assist in making minimum viable product and assessed various ways to start the production and hit the market. In other words, accelerators help to speed up the initial business process.

Incubation and acceleration process help an aspiring or a start-up to overcome initial hurdles of business. Initial stages of business must be well guided. This minimises the chances of failure. This is a great way to overcome the phobia of business or entrepreneurship. This helped many aspiring start-ups to set their business in a proper way. Proper mentorship received during the incubation process is another important factor. Overall, this acts as a good handshake deal for a start-up and its founders.

Making A Proper Business plan

Business plan is very important stage of business. It is called the blueprint of future action. Benjamin Franklin said, "if you fail to plan, you plan to fail". Planning is important and indispensable part of business cycle.

As aspiring start-up founder, one must make proper business plan for starting the business. This is a step, in which, a business founder must spend adequate time. Initially, a professional business plan might not be required. Professional business plans are required in later stage of business. These are required for fundraising, collaboration, merger & acquisition.

For this one has to define business objective and ways of achieving those. Initially the business plan must be simple as an aspiring entrepreneur will not have the expertise of making the professional business plan. Initially the easiest way to make business plan including below three points

i. **Goal of business:** Goal of business must be described in clear terms. This makes the direction of the journey proper and well defined. All types of goal must be mentioned in this section of plan. Goals may include business goals, financial goals and operational goals. Goal must be clear and well thought. This will act as a target in coming days.

ii. **The method of attending goal:** This is the action plan. The action need to be well planned. Right plan of action is very important for achieving business goals. This must include elaborate plans. Every mode of action has to be written. This may include the purchase of machinery, fundraising, payout plans, marketing plans, operational plans and manpower plans. This is the time taking procedure. Time spent on this is worth. Methods of goal attending can make or break up business. This can be a real building block of business.

iii. **Time planning for achievement:** No plan is complete without allocation of time limit. This keeps the plan intact and time bound. This is one of the indispensable factors of plan. This can keep a watch on the progress of work. This will help to know, whether a project is on time or delayed. So, an aspiring entrepreneur must plan time-slot for the completion of each component of business plan. This also defines the efficiency of the process.

What type of planning?

Basic business plan for aspiring entrepreneur must include the above-mentioned 3 points. These points help to streamline the process of starting a business. Aspiring person must spend proper time in this phase. This face can turn the table.

I am mentioning here few points which must be worked out during the planning process.

i. **Defining the business:** This is the first step. One must define what he or she wanted to do in form of business. This is the first step. Clarity of the business concept is quite important. The business must be well defined with utmost clarity. This requires a lot of brainstorming sessions. Well defined business is easy to execute.

ii. **Demand analysis:** It is important to find. Whether you are planning to make the product or service, has got a demand or not. Demand helps a product or service to move in the market. So before getting into business, a proper demand analysis is important.

iii. **Financial planning:** Financial planning is important. This is the plan, which will help you to remain afloat in business. A proper budget planning is important. It must include income and expense and cash flow planning etc. Financial planning must include a backup strategy in form of reserve capital as well. Allocation and planning for the reserve is quite important. This can lead in tough situations. Finances is the foundation of all businesses. Overall, this foundation makes the business stand.

iv. **Contingency planning:** Business faces a lot of uncertainty. This may lead to various downtimes or financial distress. So, a contingency planning is must. This can help an entrepreneur to overcome such uncertainties. So, this planning must be done beforehand only.

v. **Operational planning:** Full plan for operation should be made before the start. This has real footsteps of business. The plan must include every aspect of business. This must include the planning for getting new materials, running plan, breakdown dealing, quality control plan, efficiency assurance plan, human resources plan, etc. Operation is when a product is made or the services are delivered. So the right planning can reduce the interruption of operations.

vi. **Marketing plan:** Once the product is made it has to be sold. Once the sale happens, the revenue starts flowing in. Marketing is important for this. Better the marketing, better will be the awareness of the product.

Better the awareness, higher are the chances of sale. So marketing at times becomes the foundation for revenue flow in a business.

vii. **Plan for legal works:** Legal works are quite important for business. So, it is important for an aspiring entrepreneur to know about this. It is always recommended to sit with a good consultant and plan for the required legal works. Right legal work is indispensable. Failing which could attract huge penalties.

viii. **Manpower planning:** Planning for manpower is quite vital. Here one need to finalise the business module. One need to decide whether the aspiring entrepreneur want to start solo or with the team. Also, how much work to be done inhouse and how much to be outsource also need to be planned. This leads to the manpower planning in short and long run. This must be done in order to have a smooth business operation.

ix. **Backup planning:** Backup planning is important in business. This is required because business might not work with a single plan. One plan might fail, so a backup plan is important. It must be done before starting up the business. Backup plan acts as a support if the initial plan fails. It also saves times for re-planning.

Why planning is important?

Not only business, but every walk of life requires planning. Planning is a steppingstone of all work. Planning is the step which makes a work to start and go on. This is a blueprint which guides us across. For a start-up or right planning is indispensable. Without planning there can be many hurdles waiting. So, it is important.

A well written business plan is a wonderful tool. For an entrepreneur it leads, their goal and track their progress.

I am, hereby, providing few points which makes the business plan important.

i. **To set a better objective:** Objectives are very important in business. Objectives for a business gives a direction to the business. This gives a clarity about the business. Long-term and short-term goals are also well taken up properly with this. Right planning creates and clarifies the objectives in a much better way. The clarity of objective is the first thing an aspiring start-up founder must look into.

ii. **Check the viability and validity of idea:** Business idea comes to mind like a flash of light. The flash must be tracked and noted. Most of the time business idea used to be a raw and crude one. Idea requires a rigorous workout to make that proper. Viability and validity of the idea need to be checked. This is a rigorous step. Here the planning plays an important part. Planning is the keynote step for the checking the viability and validity of a business idea.

iii. **Communicate the business idea:** The business idea comes to the mind of a start-up founder. This idea needs to be worked upon to make it a proper business idea. Then has to be communicated to the external world. The stakeholders could be in form of co-founders, investors, employees, bankers etc. This communication need to be in form of business plan. This clarifies the idea of business to other stakeholders. These stakeholders are the real contributors in business. Presenting the plan is important, in order to effectively communicate the business idea. This process goes well with the right business plan.

iv. **Help in critical decision making:** Business involves many critical decision making, which is quite important. This journey is the juncture of many crucial decision making. The plan helps to decide on many critical issues. While dealing with the critical issues, it is important to make correct decisions. Correct decisions are the key for business success. If one has plan in place, then he or she can easily scrutinise, whether the decision are in line with the plan or not. Many times, it might deviate in short run and in line when it comes to the long-term plans. So, this is key element for crucial decision making is the plan.

v. **Helps avoiding business mistakes:** Business is a dynamic journey. It has many ups and downs. Many times, an entrepreneur make mistake intentional or unintentional which might cost a business dearly. But if one has a proper plan on hand, then the chances of mistake can be reduced to a huge extent. Minimising mistakes also reduces potential losses. So, here also planning is the key.

vi. **Better place to handle situations:** Day in and day out, business has to face a lot of situations. Situations can be favourable, or it can be unfavourable. Everyday such situation comes before the business founder. Here also, a proper plan is important for the entrepreneur. Plan can help to check whether the situation is leading towards the goal or is it deviating. It can also help to suggest preventive and rectification actions. Also, plan acts as a basic foundation block.

vii. **Secure funding:** Funding is important for any type of business. Specially if it is related to manufacturing, scale up or expand as well. Investor would require to see the business plan first. Here the business plan is the key aspect. No investor or lender would like to interact with any business unit without a proper business plan. In other words the plan reflects your business idea in a clearer way. This helps an investor or a lender to assess the business idea in a better way.

viii. **Organise the resources well:** Resources are important for business. Business requires right organization and allocation of resources. This is the real secret of the game. This distinguishes the success. To organise and use the resources properly what is required is, the plan. The plan gives the direction to the business. The business resources utilization must be as per the plan made. Deviation must be avoided, unless an urgency comes up. Business planning keep the allocated resources for urgency or exigency as well.

ix. **Identifies the potential weakness and obstacles:** Every business has some weakness other. First thing which is important is that weakness need to be identified. Many times, it becomes difficult. If you have a proper plan with you then the identification of weakness becomes easy. Not only weakness, but it also helps to identify the forthcoming obstacles in business. So, a plan is the first and basic requirement for this. The plan acts as a guiding lamp and hence identification of weakness and obstacles becomes easy.

x. **Blueprint for action:** Planning is the blueprint of future action. This action plan acts as a guide for all work. If a plan is made, then the work becomes well organised. Well organised work gives some of the finest results. This reduces the chances of error to a great extent. Blueprint makes an organised path for all type of work.

How planning helps a start-up founder?

For a start-up founder, plan is like a Bible. This is the step which helps the founder to take every step. The planning helps a start-up founder in lot of ways.

This determines a common goal for the organization and employees.

i. **Prepare for uncertainty:** The business faces a lot of uncertainty. This type of uncertainty makes a person scared. There can be various reasons for uncertainty. Some may be internal sum may be external. Control can be there on some factors whereas some factors may be beyond control. This is quite normal in business. The planning factor plays an important role. Right planning can help to face the uncertainty in a better way. If properly planned many at times, it can give uncertainty a miss.

ii. **Creating milestones:** Right from the time a business starts, it creates milestones. This may come in form of goals targets or even budget or growth. This is a stepwise phase. Here also the role and importance of planning is worth mentioning. Milestones can be created and achieved if planned properly.

iii. **Raising funds:** Every business requires fund at some point of time it can be at the time of start, During expansion or during the regular operations. This requires a lot of preparation as investor or lender verifies a lot of credentials of the company. Right planning makes the process smooth.

iv. **Facing competition:** Every business runs on competitive environment. This is a show of free market. There are advantages as well. At times, it creates highly competitive situation. Facing this requires a lot of planning. Improper handling of this, may lead to tough time at business. Getting the business pie in a competitive environment requires a lot of efforts.

v. **Effective customer handling:** Customers are the real backbone of any business. They help to keep the business rolling. Business grows with the growth of customers. If the customers are happy, they will come back for the second purchase and also provide referrals. But handling customers are not easy. Right customer handling policy need to be formulated in a business. Here also the right planning is important.

vi. **Plan the revenue model:** The revenue is earning for business. A business needs to plan for this as well. The founder needs to determine how exactly a business need to earn. Sources of revenue need to be determined and well analysed. Every revenue source should be well analysed and identified. The revenue model of the company must be well planned.

vii. **Market placement:** Every business needs to identify the market in which it is planning to operate. The product or the service of the company need to be placed in the right market. Some research work is required prior to that. Improper market placement may lead to difficulty in selling. After due research, it must be planned. With the right planning the product can be well placed in the market.

viii. **Organizational setup:** Organizational setup is required for a business to become functional. This helps to make the business run properly. The organizational setup must be done properly and with right planning. Right setup helps the business to run smoothly. This also requires a lot of planning.

ix. **Determining the course:** Business involves a lot of activities. These can be inter-related or independent of each other. At times, these activities lose focus and become too enclosed on short-term goals. As a result, the long-term goals of business get neglected. Here the determining the right course is important. So, the goals of the company do not get neglected this is an important criterion. Planning is the best suited to handle this situation.

x. **Setting priorities:** Founder cannot do everything. So is the business. Business cannot take up everything. Right priority is important. This helps to keep the focus and keep the resources allocated to the most important task. These priorities are determined if there is a well-defined plan.

Above mentioned points are just to mention a few. Real benefit of planning can be huge. This is a great option for keeping the journey of smooth.

Types of business plan.

There are many ways of classifying the business plan. This classification help a business founder to stress on specific functionality off the plan. This keeps the plan focused on certain aspects of business.

Classification based on purpose

Based on purpose of business plan can be classified as below.

i. **Lean business plan.** This type of plans is made for taking investment or applying for loans. In other words, it displays the plan for investment. This plan focuses on various quantitative aspects of business. This includes budget forecast, business estimation, growth, market analysis etc. Here the business strategy is of utmost importance. This takes account of financial data. It takes a lot of projected sales, cash flow, income and expenditure statement etc. It also mentions growth probability. This type of plan ignores certain aspects of business like company history, team details etc. It gives a miss which are non-quantitative aspects of business. Using these type of plan, investor or lender accesses of business entity.

ii. **One page business plan.** Now as the name suggests this type of plan is brief in nature and covers all major aspects of business only. In other words, one page covers all major points of the plan. This type of plan becomes easy to understand and interpret. At times start-up or prospective start-ups wish to summarise their concepts and present it to the external world or stakeholders. This is the best plan for that purpose. This type of plan is the best for regular referral and workout. It helps to introduce the business idea to various stakeholders. It is a wonderful tool for first meet to any external stakeholders.

iii. **Formal business plan.** Formal plans are used to present a comprehensive plan of business to the external people. At times, banks ask for formal plan before sanctioning the loan application. This includes plan of business strategies, funding needed, utilization plan of funds, sales and marketing projection, profit probability, growth prospect, team raising, company history etc. Many a times professional people are also involved while making this type of plan. This type of plans is quite elaborative.

Classification based on functionality

There are certain plans made based on the functions the business too. Such kind of plans are meant for a specific function. So, such function stresses on certain aspect of business. They are made aiming certain business aspect. Such functionality depends on situation or certain phases of business.

i. **Start-up business plan:** This type of plan is meant for the start-up phase of business. These are made to plan the start of business. This type of plan puts stress on initial phase and stage of business. The plan mentions organizing product & services, plan for income and expense. Market placement and marketing plans. This puts stress on financial analysis and launch planning. This stresses on the business concept, revenue forecast and marking plan. This type of plan also stresses on business idea feasibility and validation of idea. The plan acts as a guide for starting a business.

ii. **Internal business plan:** As the name suggests, the internal business plan is meant for business unit's internal work. Generally, these plans are made for internal coordination and workflow planning. At times, there are meant for sub-specific set of work as well. For example, it can be for a new project and its execution. Internal planning and action are mentioned in this type of plan. It includes financial planning, sales actions, manpower planning, marketing analysis, cost analysis, operational reviews etc. This type of plan helps an organization with proposed action for specific project.

iii. **Operational business plan:** This is the part of internal business plan. But the focus is on operational part of business. The processes of operation, operational costs, efficiency of processes, technology costs etc are considered in this type of plan.

iv. **Growth plan:** Generally, growth plans are executed in the later stage of business. However, it is always recommended that growth plan must be done in early stage. Execution can happen later. Early planning of the growth phase helps to keep the plan at the back of the head. Growth plan in early stage helps to assemble the resources required for growth in advance. At the same time, it keeps time to review the plan many times before execution. This plan focuses on the aspect of growth, fund requirement, market-pie analysis etc. Various aspects of growth are mentioned in this type of plan

v. **Feasibility plan:** This type of plan deals with the feasibility of business. The study of business plan and the steps of making it a reality is described in this type of plan. This has steps and the plans for making the product & business feasible. A business is considered as feasible, if the customers buy the product in lieu of money. In other words, business starts earning revenue. This plan also focuses on the profitability aspect of business. This notifies the steps to cross the break event point. So, for a start-up founder this plan can be of great help.

vi. **Strategic plans:** This type of plan deal with the strategic aspect of business. These are the plans to make aspect of business. These types of plans deal with mission, vision, goal, etc. Most of these factors are attached with the long term goal of business. These are made with other plans. Results of implementation appear over a period of time.

Challenges in making a business plan.

Planning may seem like a tough work, but it is due to the challenges faced. Challenges are quite common in business and in planning.

i. **Making a head-start:** Making a head-start for planning is quite important. But this is the toughest thing to do. Many times, it is a real challenge. Converting a business idea into business plan is a humongous task. This requires a lot of brainstorming followed by trial and errors. It is quite common for start-up founders.

ii. **Noting vision on paper:** This is another challenge. Noting the vision, that too a business vision, on paper is quite challenging. This requires organization of thoughts. Initially, that may seem like a very haphazard type of work. But this is one challenge which every start-up founder faces before start.

iii. **Being concise:** Most of the time business idea are quite vast and unrefined. But plan must not be that fast. It must be to the point and in brief. This means right points should be kept and balance should be erased. Many start-up founders find it tough.

iv. **Planning financials:** Financial data is one of the pillars of business. However, while starting or before the start of business it is difficult to ascertain the numbers. The planning financials includes many micro-level plannings. This includes planning capital, planning cash flow statement, planning income and expenses, planning debt, planning allocation of resources etc. A start-up founder needs to brainstorm this to a huge extent. Right planning is the key for success of business. Financial planning must be well done.

v. **Making workable goals:** Making a workable goal are quite important. This requires a lot of brainstorming. Brainstorming and working out can be the real essence of the business. Making a goal which works, is a challenge. Goal must be in sync with the vision plant. This requires a proper workout. One can make it clear and understandable. A well-made and realistic goal must be aligned with the plan made.

vi. **Presenting pivot ready module:** Change is the law of nature. This can come in form of changes in market, consumer sentiments, technology, customer needs & preferences. Hence, plan must have provision of pivoting, in sync with the changes in environment. Right planning for pivoting must be done right from beginning.

vii. **Assessing business growth:** This is one of the biggest challenges during planning. Most of the time start-up founder does not have right expertise to assess the future growth of the business. This is quite common in the initial phases of business. Assessment of business goal is important to get ready for the challenges related to that. At the some times, start-up founder has to go for right allocation of resources.

viii. **Technological selection.** Every business need technology in some way or other. This improves the efficiency and makes the work systematic.

This is a blessing. But a start-up founder has to plan for selection of right technology. This also involves cost. User friendliness of the technology is important. This makes the way for long term action in business.

ix. **Customer demand determination:** Customer is the king. So, you have to know what the king demands. If the king demands the product you make, you are done. So, this forms an important part of planning. Before planning one need to determine the customer demand. This helps a start-up founder in long run. But this is not easy. This requires multiple surveys and thorough analysis. Demand determination helps to make the product in a proper way. This helps the product to move in the market.

x. **Setting priority:** Setting priority in business is important. Business requires proper determination of priority. This helps to make the right plan of action. So, taking the step-by-step approach depends on the right setting of priority. Wrong priority can be harmful for business.

xi. **Making phase wise strategy:** Strategy must be well made at different stages of business. Strategy of business must be meet requirements for all type of stages of business cycle. The strategy of each stage is different from other. Making phase wise strategy is a challenge at time. So, the right brainstorming and consultation must be done prior to that.

xii. **Presenting the solution:** Every business solves some problem or other. It either solves an existing problem or enhances the existing solutions. So, for founder need to present the solution in well organised way this may be challenging. A start-up has to pinpoint the solution offered. Generally, a solution consists of a lot of processes. So, while presenting the solution one must be well planned and present the same in simple and proper way.

xiii. **Determination of processes and systems:** Business is backed with many processes and systems. These are the parts of day-to-day events of business. In fact, these acts as a backbone for business. A start-up founder has to plan for processes and systems beforehand. A first-time start-up founder may find it bit challenging. But despite being challenging one has to work and plan for this

xiv. **Integrative thinking:** Most of the time a start-up founder is emotionally attached to the business idea. But they miss to analyse the customers perspective of that. Customers and investors perspective must be thought as well. So as a founder one has to think both sides. This calls for integrative thinking. So, the plan has to be made considering the wellbeing of all stakeholders of the business unit.

xv. **Making it interesting:** Planning, at times, becomes monotonous. So, making the plan interesting is important for making the it realistic and durable. This is also an art.

What happens if we do not plan.

Planning is indispensable for any business activity. Planning is the key virtue. This makes the way for smooth operation. Planning organizers work to a great extent. Many start-up founders are reluctant in planning. This might seem perfect in short run but gets impacted in long run. This is very important virtue of business cycle.

i. **Allocation of resources:** One of the main goals of planning is right allocation of resources. Without proper planning, right allocation of resources might not happen. This requires a proper planning. If the right allocation of resources does not happen then the operational processes of business might get affected and at the same time chances of wastage of resources is considerably high. Resources are the most important commodity in business. Business runs on resources. It might be in form of human resources or physical resources or even in form of time being a resource. Always remember resources are limited, so the optimum utilization is the need of the hour. Allocation in right quantity and at the right time is essential for the proper run of business. The right allocation of resources can happen if the processes are well planned, so the proper planning is important for business.

ii. **Improper cash flow:** In business, cash flow is an important factor. Cash flow management has to be preceded by proper planning. This factor gives lifeline to business. Without cash flow the business dies. This is the real factor, which must be well planned. Right planning of income and proportionate planning of expenses are important. This keeps the cash flow steady. Lack of planning leads to improper execution of cash flow. This can be a bad sign in business. So, the lack of planning leads to improper cash flow in a company.

iii. **Lack of focus:** Business must remain in focus. Right focus on long- and short-term goals. This requires a proper planning. Losing the focus is not a good option. But many a times, this happens. This may be due to various factors. But a business must immediately bring back its focus to its goal. This correction is assistant by a set plan. In case, the plan is missing bringing the focus back can be a tough task. Plan acts as a yardstick in this case. So, the absence of yardstick can make it difficult to focus on the right things.

iv. **Improper goal implementation:** A business has to set long-term and short-term goals. This is important in various phases of business. This implementation must be preceded by right planning. The goal is important for all businesses. The goal makes the business move. So, the creation of the right goal is important for any business unit. Just creation of the goal may not be of any use. One has to implement the goal in business in a right way. Every member of business need to work for this. This must be distributed in form of specific targets. This has to be done properly in order to make the goal achievable. This is a specialised phase. The right planning is the key for this. In case the planning is not done, the goal setting is bound to get impacted. If the right setting of goal is not done, then goal achievement by the business unit too becomes tough. So, the lack of planning can be a trouble in this phase.

v. **Not getting ready for forthcoming event:** We live in a dynamic world. Every moment the situation changes. This change can be in form of economic situation, geopolitical situation, government policies, social systems and customer preferences. Business needs to be ready for this. One cannot become ready by its own. Right planning is required for this. Getting ready for change is important for survival in business. Many businesses got wiped out due to this. It is indispensable for any founder to make the business ready for any type of change which may come up. This adaptation to change and getting ready for the change can only happen if there is a plan for it in place. Else the whole situation will be totally haphazard

vi. **Poor execution.** Execution is one of the indispensable factors in business. Right execution helps in getting the business model right. Poor execution is a negative trend. In business it destroys the business completely. Execution depends on planning right. Plan leads to write execution and vice versa. This is a real essence of business. The execution has to be rightly planned and must be in details. Execution helps to make the business plan into reality. Poor execution leads to improper business implementation. This becomes a wrong proposition at business.

vii. **Chances of error:** Without a plan chance of error goes quite high. The error can be troublesome for any business, The plan acts as a yardstick. It acts as a steppingstone and milestone both. Planning sets the roadmap of work. With roadmap, the error can be prevented and even checked. Also, the right plan acts as a right pathway for progress and movement. Error also degrades the quality of product or service. Error further leads to rejection of product by the end user. Error during the various processes might lead to accidents as well. The planning is the best way to reduce the error. Here the planning acts as a yard stick and route back both.

viii. **Chances of failure:** Chances of failure increases manifold if we do not plan. Plan gives a road map. In absence of roadmap the chances of travelling in right path gets low. There are high chances that the direction might get lost. This could lead to many troubles sooner or later. Wrong direction is not a good thing to move in business. Absence of plan even, reduces the chances of checking the move and the actions. This increases the chances of failure. So, no planning drives towards a definite failure.

ix. **Improper financial actions:** In absence of plan, the action might not be an organised one. Same is true for financial actions also. Improper financial actions might lead to collapse of the organization. Financial actions are very important for any business unit. These steps are the support blocks for an organization. If the right planning is not done, then all the steps of financial system will become haphazard. This includes cash management, expenditure control, income calculation, account receivable tracking, credit monitoring, filing compliances, profit analysis etc. All these financial steps are vital for business. These must be well monitored and recorded. In absence of plan, monitoring will be difficult as yardstick will be missing. Hence action at the right time cannot be raised in case of a mistake. This is a great disadvantage.

x. **Not ready for exigency:** It can come up at any point of time. This can come in many ways. Handling exigency can only happen if it is planned. Right planning for exigency happens from day one. In absence of proper plan, the plan for dealing with exigency too gets stalled. Once the exigency hits the business founder might find it difficult to deal with such situations.

xi. **Not setting long term goals:** In absence of proper plan focus will always be on the short-term goals and issues. This will lead to ignorance of long-term goals of business. The long term goals are important for scale up, expansion and fundraising exercises. This helps to take the company to the next level. If the planning is not there, then the long term goals of the company are either non-existent or poorly executed. These are high chances business unit would get engaged in day-to-day affairs and ignored long term goals.

Can planning prevent failure?

The answer is "NO". The failure is a part and parcel of business. No person on the earth can say he is in business but never failed. This is the reality of business. Now and obvious question might come up that if the failure is indispensable why should one plan? The answer can be summed up with below points.

i. It reduces the chances of failure
ii. It reduces the impact of failure
iii. It assists to face the failure in a better way
iv. It helps to rise again after a failure

Above 4 points are enough to understand the whole situation. These can really help. Failure is bound to come but planning acts as a positive element in the whole process. This is a real essence of business.

Let us understand all 4 points in details:

i. **It reduces the chances of failure:** As I have mentioned the plan, gives a goal and a road map. This keeps the journey of entrepreneurship organised. At the same time, it keeps an option of monitoring the journey. Right monitoring helps to detect the deviation from the standards. This is the real motive of planning. So, with all these in place, the regular monitoring can happen. So, the causes of failure can be detected before it can cause an impact. Hence the chances of failure can be minimised to a huge extent.

ii. **It reduces the impact of failure:** In spite of all the precautions, failures are bound to come. This is inevitable and it is important to figure out how failure affects the business. Bigger the impact of failure. More is the damage. Hence the big impact of the failure has to be avoided. With planning one can sense the probable failure. This happens because the action gets deviated from the road map. Outcome too gets predicted in advance. This helps a business to know the probable result before getting the result. This gives a lead time to the business for getting ready. Getting ready reduces the impact of failure to a huge extent. Reducing the impact of failure is a huge matter. It can even save the business resources from getting used up unnecessarily.

iii. **It helps to face the failure in a better way:** Failure is a part of business cycle. This is one of the inevitable phases. It becomes a challenge for entrepreneur to face the failure. Here the plan can be of immense help. If the plan exists, then the impact of failure gets greatly reduced. With a right plan monitoring too becomes quite easy. It can help to scrutinise the causes of failure in a better way. At the same time, it can predict the failure as well. This in turn can help to face it well. With a plan in hand, facing an uncertainty can be relatively easy. Facing the failure requires a lot of courage. Plan helps to sort this to a huge extent.

iv. **Helps to rise again:** Rising after a fall is quite challenging. At times, failure can have an impact on the resources both monetary and non-monetary ones. Many founders find it hard to cope up with this. Here the plan can be of immense help. With an existing plan deviation can be identified. Also, one can scrutinise what went wrong. This can give a lot of inputs. Plan can act as an action plan for the next action. This next action plan can be of great help. This makes the next step, that is, to restart in an organised way. This can even be an emotional support at the time of stress.

So, it is well evident that the plan does not act as a failure proof substance. But helps to face it in a better way. The planning has a lot of other benefits as well. It acts as an important instrument for entrepreneurs. This is indispensable for all stages of entrepreneurship journey. This could even act as a guiding lamp for the journey.

Planning and fighting phobia

What is the main reason for the phobia? The lack of direction and undefined pathway! This creates a sense of uncertainty. This further generates the fear factor in long run. With planning both direction and pathway can be well made. So, the planning acts as a yardstick of action. It acts as a guide and the support for business founder. This is one of the finest ways to get organised.

An organised founder can tackle the unfavourable incidences in a proper way. It can boost the confidence as well. Confident founder can lead the organization in a better way. Better leading can be a great option for the organization. This type of leadership is a blessing.

Phobia creation is triggered by many factors. Planning helps to eliminate many factors contributing to the fear and phobias. So, plan can be a good instrument to fight phobias.

Planning can help fight a phobia in the following ways.

i. **Goal:** The plan creates a goal. The goal helps to drive the entrepreneur towards their mission. Goal makes the target feasible. Plan can help to determine the goal in form of long-term and short-term goals.

ii. **Route-map:** Plan helps to make a roadmap for the business journey. This roadmap can assist to make the steps of work in a proper way. Road map can help to lead the journey in an organised way.

iii. **Scrutiny:** The regular scrutiny of the process can be possible in case of a planned business. This scrutiny helps to rectify many errors in a time. These rectifications can help to detect any type of deviation from the plan. Scrutiny can even lead to modification of plan if required.

iv. **Detection of mistakes and deviations:** As I have already mentioned, in previous point about regular scrutiny of the plan. This leads to the detection of mistakes and deviations. This can minimize the losses to a great extent. This also minimises the chances an impact of failure. So, this is one of the key benefits.

v. **Identifying hurdles:** Plan helps to identify the forthcoming hurdles. Business is full of hurdles. Planning makes one ready for those hurdles. At times, with the right planning hurdles can be avoided as well

vi. **Managing failures:** Planning helps in scrutinising action to a huge extent. This helps to avoid failures. At the same time, it helps in facing the failure in a better way. I have already mentioned this previously.

vii. **Reduces uncertainty and unknowingness:** With proper plan in place, goal and the roadmap both are well defined. This leads to a well determined pathway for the whole journey at the same time. The regular scrutiny of the processes are effective in finding out the errors and the deviations. This reduces uncertainty and unknowing this to a huge extent.

viii. **Knowledge of time frame:** The time frame is very important factor in business. In a business assignment, extension of time frame it might cause a loss. This can be in form of monetary loss or non-monetary loss as well. So, it is important to determine the time frame at the planning stage only. The regular scrutiny must be done to ensure the project is moving as per the framework set for. With the plan, knowledge of time-frame comes up. Time frame helps to prevent a lot of loss in business.

ix. **Lesser chances of loss:** With the right goal, well determined pathway and the regular scrutiny in place, the chances of error gets greatly reduced. This makes a chance of loss quite less. This is one of the advantages of planning. This can be a great point of encouragement for many aspiring entrepreneurs.

x. **Better in managing trouble:** Trouble comes up without prior notice. So, one must be fully prepared to deal with it at all times. This makes the planning an indispensable virtue. Planning helps to manage their troubles in a better way. With plan in hand, facing trouble and coming out of it can be relatively easy. It also gives a framework for managing troubles.

xi. **Better vision for business:** Plan provides a roadmap for business founder. It helps a founder to stay focused on the set vision of the company. It helps to set the vision statement in a proper way. It also helps the business to stay in course and avoid deviations. This also helps to have a clearer vision.

xii. **Long term planning:** It is a common practice to focus on short-term issues instead of long term. This may be due to lot of issues. Day to day matters of the business take off the focus from the long-term goals of business. In business long term goals are more relevant. Plan keeps the weightage on the long term goals.

With all these points taken as a combined effort, the phobia in the mind of a founder can be fought. Phobias generate from ignorance and uncertainty. With the plan in place both can be tackled to a huge extent.

<u>Chapter 9:</u> Making A Proper Business plan !

Business plan is very important stage of business. It is called the blueprint of future action. Benjamin Franklin said, "if you fail to plan, you plan to fail". Planning is important and indispensable part of business cycle.

As aspiring start-up founder, one must make proper business plan for starting the business. This is a step, in which, a business founder must spend adequate time. Initially, a professional business plan might not be required. Professional business plans are required in later stage of business. These are required for fundraising, collaboration, merger & acquisition.

For this one has to define business objective and ways of achieving those. Initially the business plan must be simple as an aspiring entrepreneur will not have the expertise of making the professional business plan. Initially the easiest way to make business plan including below three points

i.   **Goal of business:** Goal of business must be described in clear terms. This makes the direction of the journey proper and well defined. All types of goal must be mentioned in this section of plan. Goals may include business goals, financial goals and operational goals. Goal must be clear and well thought. This will act as a target in coming days.

ii. **The method of attending goal:** This is the action plan. The action need to be well planned. Right plan of action is very important for achieving business goals. This must include elaborate plans. Every mode of action has to be written. This may include the purchase of machinery, fundraising, payout plans, marketing plans, operational plans and manpower plans. This is the time taking procedure. Time spent on this is worth. Methods of goal attending can make or break up business. This can be a real building block of business.

iii. **Time planning for achievement:** No plan is complete without allocation of time limit. This keeps the plan intact and time bound. This is one of the indispensable factors of plan. This can keep a watch on the progress of work. This will help to know, whether a project is on time or delayed. So, an aspiring entrepreneur must plan time-slot for the completion of each component of business plan. This also defines the efficiency of the process.

What type of planning?

Basic business plan for aspiring entrepreneur must include the above-mentioned 3 points. These points help to streamline the process of starting a business. Aspiring person must spend proper time in this phase. This face can turn the table.

I am mentioning here few points which must be worked out during the planning process.

i.   **Defining the business:** This is the first step. One must define what he or she wanted to do in form of business. This is the first step. Clarity of the business concept is quite important. The business must be well defined with utmost clarity. This requires a lot of brainstorming sessions. Well defined business is easy to execute.

ii. **Demand analysis:** It is important to find. Whether you are planning to make the product or service, has got a demand or not. Demand helps a product or service to move in the market. So before getting into business, a proper demand analysis is important.

iii. **Financial planning:** Financial planning is important. This is the plan, which will help you to remain afloat in business. A proper budget planning is important. It must include income and expense and cash flow planning etc. Financial planning must include a backup strategy in form of reserve capital as well. Allocation and planning for the reserve is quite important. This can lead in tough situations. Finances is the foundation of all businesses. Overall, this foundation makes the business stand.

iv. **Contingency planning:** Business faces a lot of uncertainty. This may lead to various downtimes or financial distress. So, a contingency planning is must. This can help an entrepreneur to overcome such uncertainties. So, this planning must be done beforehand only.

v. **Operational planning:** Full plan for operation should be made before the start. This has real footsteps of business. The plan must include every aspect of business. This must include the planning for getting new materials, running plan, breakdown dealing, quality control plan, efficiency assurance plan, human resources plan, etc. Operation is when a product is made or the services are delivered. So the right planning can reduce the interruption of operations.

vi. **Marketing plan:** Once the product is made it has to be sold. Once the sale happens, the revenue starts flowing in. Marketing is important for this. Better the marketing, better will be the awareness of the product. Better the awareness, higher are the chances of sale. So marketing at times becomes the foundation for revenue flow in a business.

vii. **Plan for legal works:** Legal works are quite important for business. So, it is important for an aspiring entrepreneur to know about this. It is always recommended to sit with a good consultant and plan for the required legal works. Right legal work is indispensable. Failing which could attract huge penalties.

viii. **Manpower planning:** Planning for manpower is quite vital. Here one need to finalise the business module. One need to decide whether the aspiring entrepreneur want to start solo or with the team. Also, how much work to be done inhouse and how much to be outsource also need to be planned. This leads to the manpower planning in short and long run. This must be done in order to have a smooth business operation.

ix. **Backup planning:** Backup planning is important in business. This is required because business might not work with a single plan. One plan might fail, so a backup plan is important. It must be done before starting up the business. Backup plan acts as a support if the initial plan fails. It also saves times for re-planning.

Why planning is important?

Not only business, but every walk of life requires planning. Planning is a steppingstone of all work. Planning is the step which makes a work to start and go on. This is a blueprint which guides us across. For a start-up or right planning is indispensable. Without planning there can be many hurdles waiting. So, it is important.

A well written business plan is a wonderful tool. For an entrepreneur it leads, their goal and track their progress.

I am, hereby, providing few points which makes the business plan important.

i. **To set a better objective:** Objectives are very important in business. Objectives for a business gives a direction to the business. This gives a clarity about the business. Long-term and short-term goals are also well taken up properly with this. Right planning creates and clarifies the objectives in a much better way. The clarity of objective is the first thing an aspiring start-up founder must look into.

ii. **Check the viability and validity of idea:** Business idea comes to mind like a flash of light. The flash must be tracked and noted. Most of the time business idea used to be a raw and crude one. Idea requires a rigorous workout to make that proper. Viability and validity of the idea need to be checked. This is a rigorous step. Here the planning plays an important part. Planning is the keynote step for the checking the viability and validity of a business idea.

iii. **Communicate the business idea:** The business idea comes to the mind of a start-up founder. This idea needs to be worked upon to make it a proper business idea. Then has to be communicated to the external world. The stakeholders could be in form of co-founders, investors, employees, bankers etc. This communication need to be in form of business plan. This clarifies the idea of business to other stakeholders. These stakeholders are the real contributors in business. Presenting the plan is important, in order to effectively communicate the business idea. This process goes well with the right business plan.

iv. **Help in critical decision making:** Business involves many critical decision making, which is quite important. This journey is the juncture of many crucial decision making. The plan helps to decide on many critical issues. While dealing with the critical issues, it is important to make correct decisions. Correct decisions are the key for business success. If one has plan in place, then he or she can easily scrutinise, whether the decision are in line with the plan or not. Many times, it might deviate in short run and in line when it comes to the long-term plans. So, this is key element for crucial decision making is the plan.

v. **Helps avoiding business mistakes:** Business is a dynamic journey. It has many ups and downs. Many times, an entrepreneur make mistake intentional or unintentional which might cost a business dearly. But if one has a proper plan on hand, then the chances of mistake can be reduced to a huge extent. Minimising mistakes also reduces potential losses. So, here also planning is the key.

vi. **Better place to handle situations:** Day in and day out, business has to face a lot of situations. Situations can be favourable, or it can be unfavourable. Everyday such situation comes before the business founder. Here also, a proper plan is important for the entrepreneur. Plan can help to check whether the situation is leading towards the goal or is it deviating. It can also help to suggest preventive and rectification actions. Also, plan acts as a basic foundation block.

vii. **Secure funding:** Funding is important for any type of business. Specially if it is related to manufacturing, scale up or expand as well. Investor would require to see the business plan first. Here the business plan is the key aspect. No investor or lender would like to interact with any business unit without a proper business plan. In other words the plan reflects your business idea in a clearer way. This helps an investor or a lender to assess the business idea in a better way.

viii. **Organise the resources well:** Resources are important for business. Business requires right organization and allocation of resources. This is the real secret of the game. This distinguishes the success. To organise and use the resources properly what is required is, the plan. The plan gives the direction to the business. The business resources utilization must be as per the plan made. Deviation must be avoided, unless an urgency comes up. Business planning keep the allocated resources for urgency or exigency as well.

ix. **Identifies the potential weakness and obstacles:** Every business has some weakness other. First thing which is important is that weakness need to be identified. Many times, it becomes difficult. If you have a proper plan with you then the identification of weakness becomes easy. Not only weakness, but it also helps to identify the forthcoming obstacles in business. So, a plan is the first and basic requirement for this. The plan acts as a guiding lamp and hence identification of weakness and obstacles becomes easy.

x. **Blueprint for action:** Planning is the blueprint of future action. This action plan acts as a guide for all work. If a plan is made, then the work becomes well organised. Well organised work gives some of the finest results. This reduces the chances of error to a great extent. Blueprint makes an organised path for all type of work.

How planning helps a start-up founder?

For a start-up founder, plan is like a Bible. This is the step which helps the founder to take every step. The planning helps a start-up founder in lot of ways.

This determines a common goal for the organization and employees.

i. **Prepare for uncertainty:** The business faces a lot of uncertainty. This type of uncertainty makes a person scared. There can be various reasons for uncertainty. Some may be internal sum may be external. Control can be there on some factors whereas some factors may be beyond control. This is quite normal in business. The planning factor plays an important role. Right planning can help to face the uncertainty in a better way. If properly planned many at times, it can give uncertainty a miss.

ii. **Creating milestones:** Right from the time a business starts, it creates milestones. This may come in form of goals targets or even budget or growth. This is a stepwise phase. Here also the role and importance of planning is worth mentioning. Milestones can be created and achieved if planned properly.

iii. **Raising funds:** Every business requires fund at some point of time it can be at the time of start, During expansion or during the regular operations. This requires a lot of preparation as investor or lender verifies a lot of credentials of the company. Right planning makes the process smooth.

iv. **Facing competition:** Every business runs on competitive environment. This is a show of free market. There are advantages as well. At times, it creates highly competitive situation. Facing this requires a lot of planning. Improper handling of this, may lead to tough time at business. Getting the business pie in a competitive environment requires a lot of efforts.

v. **Effective customer handling:** Customers are the real backbone of any business. They help to keep the business rolling. Business grows with the growth of customers. If the customers are happy, they will come back for the second purchase and also provide referrals. But handling customers are not easy. Right customer handling policy need to be formulated in a business. Here also the right planning is important.

vi. **Plan the revenue model:** The revenue is earning for business. A business needs to plan for this as well. The founder needs to determine how exactly a business need to earn. Sources of revenue need to be determined and well analysed. Every revenue source should be well analysed and identified. The revenue model of the company must be well planned.

vii. **Market placement:** Every business needs to identify the market in which it is planning to operate. The product or the service of the company need to be placed in the right market. Some research work is required prior to that. Improper market placement may lead to difficulty in selling. After due research, it must be planned. With the right planning the product can be well placed in the market.

viii. **Organizational setup:** Organizational setup is required for a business to become functional. This helps to make the business run properly. The organizational setup must be done properly and with right planning. Right setup helps the business to run smoothly. This also requires a lot of planning.

ix. **Determining the course:** Business involves a lot of activities. These can be inter-related or independent of each other. At times, these activities lose focus and become too enclosed on short-term goals. As a result, the long-term goals of business get neglected. Here the determining the right course is important. So, the goals of the company do not get neglected this is an important criterion. Planning is the best suited to handle this situation.

x. **Setting priorities:** Founder cannot do everything. So is the business. Business cannot take up everything. Right priority is important. This helps to keep the focus and keep the resources allocated to the most important task. These priorities are determined if there is a well-defined plan.

Above mentioned points are just to mention a few. Real benefit of planning can be huge. This is a great option for keeping the journey of smooth.

Types of business plan.

There are many ways of classifying the business plan. This classification help a business founder to stress on specific functionality off the plan. This keeps the plan focused on certain aspects of business.

Classification based on purpose

Based on purpose of business plan can be classified as below.

i. **Lean business plan.** This type of plans is made for taking investment or applying for loans. In other words, it displays the plan for investment. This plan focuses on various quantitative aspects of business. This includes budget forecast, business estimation, growth, market analysis etc. Here the business strategy is of utmost importance. This takes account of financial data. It takes a lot of projected sales, cash flow, income and expenditure statement etc. It also mentions growth probability. This type of plan ignores certain aspects of business like company history, team details etc. It gives a miss which are non-quantitative aspects of business. Using these type of plan, investor or lender accesses of business entity.

ii. **One page business plan.** Now as the name suggests this type of plan is brief in nature and covers all major aspects of business only. In other words, one page covers all major points of the plan. This type of plan becomes easy to understand and interpret. At times start-up or prospective start-ups wish to summarise their concepts and present it to the external world or stakeholders. This is the best plan for that purpose. This type of plan is the best for regular referral and workout. It helps to introduce the business idea to various stakeholders. It is a wonderful tool for first meet to any external stakeholders.

iii. **Formal business plan.** Formal plans are used to present a comprehensive plan of business to the external people. At times, banks ask for formal plan before sanctioning the loan application. This includes plan of business strategies, funding needed, utilization plan of funds, sales and marketing projection, profit probability, growth prospect, team raising, company history etc. Many a times professional people are also involved while making this type of plan. This type of plans is quite elaborative.

Classification based on functionality

There are certain plans made based on the functions the business too. Such kind of plans are meant for a specific function. So, such function stresses on certain aspect of business. They are made aiming certain business aspect. Such functionality depends on situation or certain phases of business.

i. **Start-up business plan:** This type of plan is meant for the start-up phase of business. These are made to plan the start of business. This type of plan puts stress on initial phase and stage of business. The plan mentions organizing product & services, plan for income and expense. Market placement and marketing plans. This puts stress on financial analysis and launch planning. This stresses on the business concept, revenue forecast and marking plan. This type of plan also stresses on business idea feasibility and validation of idea. The plan acts as a guide for starting a business.

ii. **Internal business plan:** As the name suggests, the internal business plan is meant for business unit's internal work. Generally, these plans are made for internal coordination and workflow planning. At times, there are meant for sub-specific set of work as well. For example, it can be for a new project and its execution. Internal planning and action are mentioned in this type of plan. It includes financial planning, sales actions, manpower planning, marketing analysis, cost analysis, operational reviews etc. This type of plan helps an organization with proposed action for specific project.

iii. **Operational business plan:** This is the part of internal business plan. But the focus is on operational part of business. The processes of operation, operational costs, efficiency of processes, technology costs etc are considered in this type of plan.

iv. **Growth plan:** Generally, growth plans are executed in the later stage of business. However, it is always recommended that growth plan must be done in early stage. Execution can happen later. Early planning of the growth phase helps to keep the plan at the back of the head. Growth plan in early stage helps to assemble the resources required for growth in advance. At the same time, it keeps time to review the plan many times before execution. This plan focuses on the aspect of growth, fund requirement, market-pie analysis etc. Various aspects of growth are mentioned in this type of plan

v. **Feasibility plan:** This type of plan deals with the feasibility of business. The study of business plan and the steps of making it a reality is described in this type of plan. This has steps and the plans for making the product & business feasible. A business is considered as feasible, if the customers buy the product in lieu of money. In other words, business starts earning revenue. This plan also focuses on the profitability aspect of business. This notifies the steps to cross the break event point. So, for a start-up founder this plan can be of great help.

vi. **Strategic plans:** This type of plan deal with the strategic aspect of business. These are the plans to make aspect of business. These types of plans deal with mission, vision, goal, etc. Most of these factors are attached with the long term goal of business. These are made with other plans. Results of implementation appear over a period of time.

Challenges in making a business plan.
Planning may seem like a tough work, but it is due to the challenges faced. Challenges are quite common in business and in planning.

i. **Making a head-start:** Making a head-start for planning is quite important. But this is the toughest thing to do. Many times, it is a real challenge. Converting a business idea into business plan is a humongous task. This requires a lot of brainstorming followed by trial and errors. It is quite common for start-up founders.

ii. **Noting vision on paper:** This is another challenge. Noting the vision, that too a business vision, on paper is quite challenging. This requires organization of thoughts. Initially, that may seem like a very haphazard type of work. But this is one challenge which every start-up founder faces before start.

iii. **Being concise:** Most of the time business idea are quite vast and unrefined. But plan must not be that fast. It must be to the point and in brief. This means right points should be kept and balance should be erased. Many start-up founders find it tough.

iv. **Planning financials:** Financial data is one of the pillars of business. However, while starting or before the start of business it is difficult to ascertain the numbers. The planning financials includes many micro-level plannings. This includes planning capital, planning cash flow statement, planning income and expenses, planning debt, planning allocation of resources etc. A start-up founder needs to brainstorm this to a huge extent. Right planning is the key for success of business. Financial planning must be well done.

v. **Making workable goals:** Making a workable goal are quite important. This requires a lot of brainstorming. Brainstorming and working out can be the real essence of the business. Making a goal which works, is a challenge. Goal must be in sync with the vision plant. This requires a proper workout. One can make it clear and understandable. A well-made and realistic goal must be aligned with the plan made.

vi. **Presenting pivot ready module:** Change is the law of nature. This can come in form of changes in market, consumer sentiments, technology, customer needs & preferences. Hence, plan must have provision of pivoting, in sync with the changes in environment. Right planning for pivoting must be done right from beginning.

vii. **Assessing business growth:** This is one of the biggest challenges during planning. Most of the time start-up founder does not have right expertise to assess the future growth of the business. This is quite common in the initial phases of business. Assessment of business goal is important to get ready for the challenges related to that. At the some times, start-up founder has to go for right allocation of resources.

viii. **Technological selection.** Every business need technology in some way or other. This improves the efficiency and makes the work systematic. This is a blessing. But a start-up founder has to plan for selection of right technology. This also involves cost. User friendliness of the technology is important. This makes the way for long term action in business.

ix. **Customer demand determination:** Customer is the king. So, you have to know what the king demands. If the king demands the product you make, you are done. So, this forms an important part of planning. Before planning one need to determine the customer demand. This helps a start-up founder in long run. But this is not easy. This requires multiple surveys and thorough analysis. Demand determination helps to make the product in a proper way. This helps the product to move in the market.

x. **Setting priority:** Setting priority in business is important. Business requires proper determination of priority. This helps to make the right plan of action. So, taking the step-by-step approach depends on the right setting of priority. Wrong priority can be harmful for business.

xi. **Making phase wise strategy:** Strategy must be well made at different stages of business. Strategy of business must be meet requirements for all type of stages of business cycle. The strategy of each stage is different from other. Making phase wise strategy is a challenge at time. So, the right brainstorming and consultation must be done prior to that.

xii. **Presenting the solution:** Every business solves some problem or other. It either solves an existing problem or enhances the existing solutions. So, for founder need to present the solution in well organised way this may be challenging. A start-up has to pinpoint the solution offered. Generally, a solution consists of a lot of processes. So, while presenting the solution one must be well planned and present the same in simple and proper way.

xiii. **Determination of processes and systems:** Business is backed with many processes and systems. These are the parts of day-to-day events of business. In fact, these acts as a backbone for business. A start-up founder has to plan for processes and systems beforehand. A first-time start-up founder may find it bit challenging. But despite being challenging one has to work and plan for this

xiv. **Integrative thinking:** Most of the time a start-up founder is emotionally attached to the business idea. But they miss to analyse the customers perspective of that. Customers and investors perspective must be thought as well. So as a founder one has to think both sides. This calls for integrative thinking. So, the plan has to be made considering the wellbeing of all stakeholders of the business unit.

xv. **Making it interesting:** Planning, at times, becomes monotonous. So, making the plan interesting is important for making the it realistic and durable. This is also an art.

What happens if we do not plan.

Planning is indispensable for any business activity. Planning is the key virtue. This makes the way for smooth operation. Planning organizers work to a great extent. Many start-up founders are reluctant in planning. This might seem perfect in short run but gets impacted in long run. This is very important virtue of business cycle.

i. **Allocation of resources:** One of the main goals of planning is right allocation of resources. Without proper planning, right allocation of resources might not happen. This requires a proper planning. If the right allocation of resources does not happen then the operational processes of business might get affected and at the same time chances of wastage of resources is considerably high. Resources are the most important commodity in business. Business runs on resources. It might be in form of human resources or physical resources or even in form of time being a resource. Always remember resources are limited, so the optimum utilization is the need of the hour. Allocation in right quantity and at the right time is essential for the proper run of business. The right allocation of resources can happen if the processes are well planned, so the proper planning is important for business.

ii. **Improper cash flow:** In business, cash flow is an important factor. Cash flow management has to be preceded by proper planning. This factor gives lifeline to business. Without cash flow the business dies. This is the real factor, which must be well planned. Right planning of income and proportionate planning of expenses are important. This keeps the cash flow steady. Lack of planning leads to improper execution of cash flow. This can be a bad sign in business. So, the lack of planning leads to improper cash flow in a company.

iii. **Lack of focus:** Business must remain in focus. Right focus on long- and short-term goals. This requires a proper planning. Losing the focus is not a good option. But many a times, this happens. This may be due to various factors. But a business must immediately bring back its focus to its goal. This correction is assistant by a set plan. In case, the plan is missing bringing the focus back can be a tough task. Plan acts as a yardstick in this case. So, the absence of yardstick can make it difficult to focus on the right things.

iv. **Improper goal implementation:** A business has to set long-term and short-term goals. This is important in various phases of business. This implementation must be preceded by right planning. The goal is important for all businesses. The goal makes the business move. So, the creation of the right goal is important for any business unit. Just creation of the goal may not be of any use. One has to implement the goal in business in a right way. Every member of business need to work for this. This must be distributed in form of specific targets. This has to be done properly in order to make the goal achievable. This is a specialised phase. The right planning is the key for this. In case the planning is not done, the goal setting is bound to get impacted. If the right setting of goal is not done, then goal achievement by the business unit too becomes tough. So, the lack of planning can be a trouble in this phase.

v. **Not getting ready for forthcoming event:** We live in a dynamic world. Every moment the situation changes. This change can be in form of economic situation, geopolitical situation, government policies, social systems and customer preferences. Business needs to be ready for this. One cannot become ready by its own. Right planning is required for this. Getting ready for change is important for survival in business. Many businesses got wiped out due to this. It is indispensable for any founder to make the business ready for any type of change which may come up. This adaptation to change and getting ready for the change can only happen if there is a plan for it in place. Else the whole situation will be totally haphazard

vi. **Poor execution.** Execution is one of the indispensable factors in business. Right execution helps in getting the business model right. Poor execution is a negative trend. In business it destroys the business completely. Execution depends on planning right. Plan leads to write execution and vice versa. This is a real essence of business. The execution has to be rightly planned and must be in details. Execution helps to make the business plan into reality. Poor execution leads to improper business implementation. This becomes a wrong proposition at business.

vii. **Chances of error:** Without a plan chance of error goes quite high. The error can be troublesome for any business, The plan acts as a yardstick. It acts as a steppingstone and milestone both. Planning sets the roadmap of work. With roadmap, the error can be prevented and even checked. Also, the right plan acts as a right pathway for progress and movement. Error also degrades the quality of product or service. Error further leads to rejection of product by the end user. Error during the various processes might lead to accidents as well. The planning is the best way to reduce the error. Here the planning acts as a yard stick and route back both.

viii. **Chances of failure:** Chances of failure increases manifold if we do not plan. Plan gives a road map. In absence of roadmap the chances of travelling in right path gets low. There are high chances that the direction might get lost. This could lead to many troubles sooner or later. Wrong direction is not a good thing to move in business. Absence of plan even, reduces the chances of checking the move and the actions. This increases the chances of failure. So, no planning drives towards a definite failure.

ix. **Improper financial actions:** In absence of plan, the action might not be an organised one. Same is true for financial actions also. Improper financial actions might lead to collapse of the organization. Financial actions are very important for any business unit. These steps are the support blocks for an organization. If the right planning is not done, then all the steps of financial system will become haphazard. This includes cash management, expenditure control, income calculation, account receivable tracking, credit monitoring, filing compliances, profit analysis etc. All these financial steps are vital for business. These must be well monitored and recorded. In absence of plan, monitoring will be difficult as yardstick will be missing. Hence action at the right time cannot be raised in case of a mistake. This is a great disadvantage.

x. **Not ready for exigency:** It can come up at any point of time. This can come in many ways. Handling exigency can only happen if it is planned. Right planning for exigency happens from day one. In absence of proper plan, the plan for dealing with exigency too gets stalled. Once the exigency hits the business founder might find it difficult to deal with such situations.

xi. **Not setting long term goals:** In absence of proper plan focus will always be on the short-term goals and issues. This will lead to ignorance of long-term goals of business. The long term goals are important for scale up, expansion and fundraising exercises. This helps to take the company to the next level. If the planning is not there, then the long term goals of the company are either non-existent or poorly executed. These are high chances business unit would get engaged in day-to-day affairs and ignored long term goals.

<u>Can planning prevent failure?</u>

The answer is "NO". The failure is a part and parcel of business. No person on the earth can say he is in business but never failed. This is the reality of business. Now and obvious question might come up that if the failure is indispensable why should one plan? The answer can be summed up with below points.

i. It reduces the chances of failure
ii. It reduces the impact of failure
iii. It assists to face the failure in a better way
iv. It helps to rise again after a failure

Above 4 points are enough to understand the whole situation. These can really help. Failure is bound to come but planning acts as a positive element in the whole process. This is a real essence of business.

Let us understand all 4 points in details:

i. **It reduces the chances of failure:** As I have mentioned the plan, gives a goal and a road map. This keeps the journey of entrepreneurship organised. At the same time, it keeps an option of monitoring the journey. Right monitoring helps to detect the deviation from the standards. This is the real motive of planning. So, with all these in place, the regular monitoring can happen. So, the causes of failure can be detected before it can cause an impact. Hence the chances of failure can be minimised to a huge extent.

ii. **It reduces the impact of failure:** In spite of all the precautions, failures are bound to come. This is inevitable and it is important to figure out how failure affects the business. Bigger the impact of failure. More is the damage. Hence the big impact of the failure has to be avoided. With planning one can sense the probable failure. This happens because the action gets deviated from the road map. Outcome too gets predicted in advance. This helps a business to know the probable result before getting the result. This gives a lead time to the business for getting ready. Getting ready reduces the impact of failure to a huge extent. Reducing the impact of failure is a huge matter. It can even save the business resources from getting used up unnecessarily.

iii. **It helps to face the failure in a better way:** Failure is a part of business cycle. This is one of the inevitable phases. It becomes a challenge for entrepreneur to face the failure. Here the plan can be of immense help. If the plan exists, then the impact of failure gets greatly reduced. With a right plan monitoring too becomes quite easy. It can help to scrutinise the causes of failure in a better way. At the same time, it can predict the failure as well. This in turn can help to face it well. With a plan in hand, facing an uncertainty can be relatively easy. Facing the failure requires a lot of courage. Plan helps to sort this to a huge extent.

iv. **Helps to rise again:** Rising after a fall is quite challenging. At times, failure can have an impact on the resources both monetary and non-monetary ones. Many founders find it hard to cope up with this. Here the plan can be of immense help. With an existing plan deviation can be identified. Also, one can scrutinise what went wrong. This can give a lot of inputs. Plan can act as an action plan for the next action. This next action plan can be of great help. This makes the next step, that is, to restart in an organised way. This can even be an emotional support at the time of stress.

So, it is well evident that the plan does not act as a failure proof substance. But helps to face it in a better way. The planning has a lot of other benefits as well. It acts as an important instrument for entrepreneurs. This is indispensable for all stages of entrepreneurship journey. This could even act as a guiding lamp for the journey.

Planning and fighting phobia

What is the main reason for the phobia? The lack of direction and undefined pathway! This creates a sense of uncertainty. This further generates the fear factor in long run. With planning both direction and pathway can be well made. So, the planning acts as a yardstick of action. It acts as a guide and the support for business founder. This is one of the finest ways to get organised.

An organised founder can tackle the unfavourable incidences in a proper way. It can boost the confidence as well. Confident founder can lead the organization in a better way. Better leading can be a great option for the organization. This type of leadership is a blessing.

Phobia creation is triggered by many factors. Planning helps to eliminate many factors contributing to the fear and phobias. So, plan can be a good instrument to fight phobias.

Planning can help fight a phobia in the following ways.

i. **Goal:** The plan creates a goal. The goal helps to drive the entrepreneur towards their mission. Goal makes the target feasible. Plan can help to determine the goal in form of long-term and short-term goals.

ii. **Route-map:** Plan helps to make a roadmap for the business journey. This roadmap can assist to make the steps of work in a proper way. Road map can help to lead the journey in an organised way.

iii. **Scrutiny:** The regular scrutiny of the process can be possible in case of a planned business. This scrutiny helps to rectify many errors in a time. These rectifications can help to detect any type of deviation from the plan. Scrutiny can even lead to modification of plan if required.

iv. **Detection of mistakes and deviations:** As I have already mentioned, in previous point about regular scrutiny of the plan. This leads to the detection of mistakes and deviations. This can minimize the losses to a great extent. This also minimises the chances an impact of failure. So, this is one of the key benefits.

v. **Identifying hurdles:** Plan helps to identify the forthcoming hurdles. Business is full of hurdles. Planning makes one ready for those hurdles. At times, with the right planning hurdles can be avoided as well

vi. **Managing failures:** Planning helps in scrutinising action to a huge extent. This helps to avoid failures. At the same time, it helps in facing the failure in a better way. I have already mentioned this previously.

vii. **Reduces uncertainty and unknowingness:** With proper plan in place, goal and the roadmap both are well defined. This leads to a well determined pathway for the whole journey at the same time. The regular scrutiny of the processes are effective in finding out the errors and the deviations. This reduces uncertainty and unknowing this to a huge extent.

viii. **Knowledge of time frame:** The time frame is very important factor in business. In a business assignment, extension of time frame it might cause a loss. This can be in form of monetary loss or non-monetary loss as well. So, it is important to determine the time frame at the planning stage only. The regular scrutiny must be done to ensure the project is moving as per the framework set for. With the plan, knowledge of time-frame comes up. Time frame helps to prevent a lot of loss in business.

ix. **Lesser chances of loss:** With the right goal, well determined pathway and the regular scrutiny in place, the chances of error gets greatly reduced. This makes a chance of loss quite less. This is one of the advantages of planning. This can be a great point of encouragement for many aspiring entrepreneurs.

x. **Better in managing trouble:** Trouble comes up without prior notice. So, one must be fully prepared to deal with it at all times. This makes the planning an indispensable virtue. Planning helps to manage their troubles in a better way. With plan in hand, facing trouble and coming out of it can be relatively easy. It also gives a framework for managing troubles.

xi. **Better vision for business:** Plan provides a roadmap for business founder. It helps a founder to stay focused on the set vision of the company. It helps to set the vision statement in a proper way. It also helps the business to stay in course and avoid deviations. This also helps to have a clearer vision.

xii. **Long term planning:** It is a common practice to focus on short-term issues instead of long term. This may be due to lot of issues. Day to day matters of the business take off the focus from the long-term goals of business. In business long term goals are more relevant. Plan keeps the weightage on the long term goals.

With all these points taken as a combined effort, the phobia in the mind of a founder can be fought. Phobias generate from ignorance and uncertainty. With the plan in place both can be tackled to a huge extent.

CHAPTER X

Psychological Price

For any journey, price is indispensable. Same is true with the business journey as well. Business requires a lot of prices which one pays being an entrepreneur. This price does not refer to the monetary price always. Instead, a lot of non-monetary prices are also paid. There are lot of non-monetary prices which come up during the course of journey. Psychological price is one such non-monetary price. Every entrepreneur has to pay a psychological price of running a business. This concept became a much talk subject following an article by Jessica Bruder. This article won an award in magazine personal service category in 2014 annual award contest of deadline club - the New York City chapter of Society of professional journalists.

Here the psychological price refers to all types of mental anxieties which an entrepreneur goes through. It is quite difficult to measure the impact of this. Such type of prices needs to be assessed. This depends on person to person and from time to time. This price includes everything. Right from waking up in the morning, arranging funds, stress of meeting, panic due to unforeseen conditions, untimely eating habits, late night work, excess screentime etc. All these take a toll on the business founder.

However, hardship is indispensable for business success. Every founder has to do a lot of hardship for the business. These hardships too contribute to the psychological price.

Most interesting part of the psychological price is that it cannot be measured in numerical. There is no unit for this. Also, this is a relative in nature. For the same type of hardship, the price paid varies from person to person. This makes the price bit complicated in a way. Despite all types of complications every founder must be ready to face this. Not considering this component can be a bad proposition. This might lead to the burnout phase and subsequently to other complications. So, the best way to deal with it is to find the price and get ready for it.

What takes the price?

This question is quite common. Many ask why a psychological price tag is added to the journey of entrepreneurship. There are many aspects of entrepreneurship which takes a toll on the entrepreneur. This is quite common.

These factors can be different for different people. At the same time extent of impact is also different. Certain factors impacts more to certain people and vice versa. This is more of a relative factor. The journey is full of thorns.

I am mentioning here few common factors.

i. **Unique business problems:** The business itself is a problem-solving avenue. It solves certain problem or enhances the solutions. But every business faces certain unique problems. These problems start from inception of business or at times even before. These problems are specific for specific types of businesses. These problems start at the idea stage. This is the phase when the founders of the company are without any resource. So, every problem has to be dealt by themselves. Big problem faced during this stage is validating the business idea. Most of the time, founders think their ideas are great. But this might be otherwise. This is another unique problem. Validating and refining the business idea is very consuming process. It consumes time, energy and causes fatigue at certain point of time. Unique problems are indispensable. They are sure to arrive. These unique problems take long time to get sorted. At times, solving everything might not be even possible. Many proprietary issues too come up. At times, managing co-founders too become a tedious task. Finalising the portfolio of co-founder is a very elaborate task. Co-founders are important components of a business. So, this need to be checked and sorted. These are another sort of unique problem founder gets entangled with. These types of problems are quite common. This is one of the factors which takes the psychological price.

ii. **Business ecosystem:** Business run in an ecosystem. Business cannot be done in isolation. This includes all factors contributing to a business cycle. This can be an easy question that how ecosystem can lead to pay the psychological price. Answer can be tricky and confusing. But it is interesting to understand. Many factors are required for business to perform their day-to-day Work. Each factors have their own way to operate and have own set of problems. A founder has to sort all problems and make a business fit in the ecosystem. This is one of the toughest jobs. This requires rigorous exercise. This needs a lot of time and hard work. This is ongoing process. Keeping the business ecosystem intact is a continuous job. This goes on throughout the life cycle of a business. Regular workout, brainstorming and strategization is required. Once a business is placed in the ecosystem next challenge is to keep it in a system. Many challenges come up with this. This may be in form of operational issue, financial problem, various contingencies, operational matters etc. All these factors need to be dealt with in order to keep pace with the ecosystem factors. Many a times many external factors too affects the placement of business in ecosystem.

iii. **Lonely journey:** The journey of entrepreneurship is quite lonely. A business founder has to take the decisions by himself. Most of the problem are also to be addressed by himself. Many a times and entrepreneur follow his vision alone as the people surrounding cannot understand or relate with the vision. This is the most disturbing part of journey. Making others convinced about the vision with business proposition creates a virtual loneliness. This situation is like surrounded by people but still lonely. This situation is quite common in the journey of entrepreneurship. There are many instances. This lonely journey comes mainly due to the fact that entrepreneur's journey is bit different from the common crowd. Result are the thoughts and the actions to get bit different. Distinguishes the part of business founder. This creates a vacuum for the business founder. It also creates an emotional vacuum. Most of the time people are not attached with the founder's emotional setup. This emotional vacuum is also quite depressing, at times. At the same time, the journey of entrepreneurship is full of failures. Entrepreneurs do need to face this by himself or herself many times have entrepreneur do not get people next to them. This also eats up entrepreneur emotionally. All the lonely journey of entrepreneurship takes toll on the life of the founder.

iv. **The pressure to perform:** When the founder decides to start a venture, the chances of failure of the venture is quite high. This affects and rocks the subconscious mind. Further this puts them in extreme pressure to perform. The pressure to perform takes a toll. The pressure to perform is quite high at times. Society too adds to the pressure. When a founder takes off-route from the one-way flowing society, there are more eyeballs on that person. This adds a huge psychological pressure on the founder. At times, this situation turns quite stressful. This makes a founder to work unusually long and under stressful environment. This is the real psychological stress for him or her.

v. **No cut off switch:** Unlike a regular job, entrepreneurship journey does not have a cut-off switch. This is a peculiar instance of business. This has unlike a salaried job, wherein a person cuts off after a certain time. A business founder cannot do that. He or she is the base and the face of the business. His vision gets to the vision of business. He is the final point of escalation. Founder cannot cut off from this. Business at any point of time requires founders to get involved. This can lead to excessive of the stress at some point of time. This is a regular phenomenon with business founders.

vi. **Failure - an inevitable scenario:** In business failure is inevitable. No one in this planet can stop this. Every entrepreneur fails at some point of time or other. It is a common phenomenon. Failure takes a toll on the business founder. At times, the failure leads to a lot of damages in form of monetary resources, work hour, physical and mental exhaustion as well. All these are faced by entrepreneur in a big way. At times, they become answerable to various people like investors, co-founders, bankers, board-member. Facing this may not be an easy task. Answering the queries and other aspects are also quite tough. The failure is one of the virtues which comes in some stage or other. Entrepreneur must deal with it.

vii. **Responsibility of a team:** A founder always has the responsibility of his or her team. In spite of all problems or hurdles, team has to be taken care of. Their salary perks and other commitment need to be dispersed facing all odds. Whether it is a profit or loss, team need to be taken care well. All problems of the team have to be sorted and all escalations to be handled in a proper way. All these might seem easy, but it is not. Meanwhile if anything goes wrong, the penalty of that has to be borne by the founder. All these are quite troublesome for a founder over a period of time. At start-up stage, when the resources are limited, handling the team causes can lead to a lot of stress. These factors take a toll on the founder.

viii. **Responsibility of all actions:** A founder has to take responsibility of all actions of business. All good and bad actions responsibility has to be taken by the founder only. Unlike an employee, a founder cannot pass the buck and avoid responsibility. This is a unique situation for business founders. This make a tough time for the owners at times. Even if the founder is not directly involved in certain actions still the responsibility comes up. These types of responsibilities are quite worrisome for a founder. These take psychological toll over a period of time.

ix. **Buck stops at founder:** In an organization all escalations finally stop at founder. These are really stressful. The founder at the end of the day owns final responsibility of all actions related to business. Employees can pass the buck mostly to their seniors but business founder do not have that option. He or she had to own every action and its consequences. Buck comes in form of customer complaints, audit issues, legal matters, inventory management, investor query, lender decisions, operational issues, security threats etc. The list is quite endless. But these stop at the founder finally. Founder is the final authority of all type of escalations. Most of the time escalation which come up to the founder are complicated and tough to handle. All these add up to the psychological price of entrepreneurship, these are stressful at times.

x. **Scrutiny by others:** A business founder is always scrutinised by a lot of people. The list of the people is endless. This includes investors, bankers, customers, government agencies, tax authorities, employees, co-founders, relatives, friends, etc. Some type of scrutiny are formal and authoritative in nature like investors, bankers, tax authorities etc. While others are informal in nature like done by relatives, friends and neighbours. Formal scrutiny happens over a defined framework. Informal scrutiny is done without any specific requirement. This many a times comes over ironical matters. But a founder faces them and deals with them. The founder faces the formal scrutiny as per that defined requirement. Informal scrutiny happens without any specific reasons. These too add up to the psychological price of entrepreneurship.

The above mentioned 10 factors are quite common. But the list is endless. These lead to some of the stressful events of business. That is the price of founder pays for business.

Health hazards

Psychological price of entrepreneurship takes a toll on business founders. This makes a great impact on the health of the founder. These health hazards are at times visible and at times not visible. But effects do happen. That's a fact and reality. Entrepreneurs suffer from a lot of lifestyle and stress related disorders. Many of those carry on for whole life. Every profession has its own health hazards. Entrepreneurship is no exception. Hence, health hazards are common results of regular psychological toll.

Here I am notifying some of the common hazards of paying psychological price.

i. **Stress:** Stress is the most common side effect of psychological price which a business founder pays. Stress is a silent killer. Stress acts as an origin point of many related disorders. The point of stress most of the time is not expressed and remains hidden in with founder. Stress is quite common with founders. Starting a business and making of business are two toughest jobs in the world. That's why everyone does not become an entrepreneur. One of the main reasons for this is they are unable to handle the stress related matters. This is the key factor. This is the first impact of entrepreneurship. As I have said, the stress can be the origin point of many a related ailment. This is quite common with business founders.

ii. **Lifestyle disorders:** Lifestyle disorders are the results of reckless lifestyle of business founders. Lifestyle disorder take a toll on business owners. There are a wide range of such disorders. Lifestyle disorders if ignored can lead to a lot of physical and mental complications. This happens irrespective of age. During the initial stages of entrepreneurship journey, a founder has to do almost every work. This may lead to a long hour - at times work during ungodly hours too. This can lead to a lot of health complications. This is another health hazard.

iii. **Sleeplessness:** This is one of the most common situations faced by the business owners. Psychological price paid has an impact on sleep and resting patterns. This is quite common amongst entrepreneurs. This is one of the results of psychological price which an entrepreneur pays. This is caused due to various reasons. This can be an outcome of certain medical conditions as well. Overall sleeplessness is one of the key outcomes of business. This has many adverse effects on one's health.

iv. **Depression:** Depression also shows up at some point of time with some business founders. The condition, most of the time, gets undetected. Depression can be because of the lonely entrepreneurship journey. Only a business founder knows the pains of business journey. Depression can even be due to the long and lonely path full of hurdles and struggles. Failure are regular companions of business journey. All these factors lead to depression. Most of the time depressions go undetected. The situations get detected only if the situation worsens. This is another psychological price.

v. **Nervous breakdown:** This happens in extreme cases. This is one of the highest price founders pays. This happens when the stress of entrepreneurship goes out of control. This is serious health issue.

Nervous breakdown requires immediate medical attention. Such type of issues can happen quite often. Most of the time founders manage to come out of the situation. However few times they require professional help and counselling. One must know the initial stages of this and must take counter measures to prevent that.

vi. **Anxiety:** Anxiety is quite common with business founders. Regular workload combined with uncertainties contribute to anxiety. This takes a toll on the business founders. Anxiety may lead to many health-related complications. Anxiety most of the time looks like silent killer. This can even lead to much health related and lifestyle disorders. Apart from that anxiety attacks are not uncommon.

vii. **Mood swings:** Mood swings are also quite common. This may happen over a certain period. Most of the time co-owners and family members detect this. Mood swings come in form of unusual behaviour and absurd reactions. Such swings may go on for quite some time. Mood swings can lead to a lot of issues for the people around.

viii. **Loss of appetite:** Loss of appetite can be a common problem and mostly goes undetected. This health problem is quite common with entrepreneurs. Loss of appetite may lead to a lot of other health related problems. Health problems show up over a period of time. If untreated it might lead to major elements. The loss of appetite may be the starting point of many stomach related issues and lifestyle disorders. Loss of appetite can be temporary or long staying. This must not be ignored for a long time.

ix. **Gastric disorders:** This is another type of disorders common with entrepreneurs. Such type of disorders is quite common. Such disorders make people quite tensed and lead to loss of productivity. Due to lifestyle such type of disorders is becoming common nowadays. If not treated properly and on time, it could lead to further complications hey.

x. **Social withdrawal:** This is the result of many related methods. Social withdrawal is rare but can be dangerous. So the social withdrawal must be diagnosed and remedial actions must be taken on time. This can lead to many psychological ailments. In later stage, this might be a cause of physical illness too. Social withdrawal might not harm a person immediately but over a period of time it can lead to other complications.

Other complications are just to name a few. There are many hazards which can be counted. These make the journey of entrepreneurship bit rough at times.

Factors leading to psychological price.

Psychological price is indispensable for founder to pay. No one can skip this. The factors leading to founder to go for psychological price are many. Ironically such factors cannot be avoided. Every business founder faces those at some point of time or other. Hence it is important for an entrepreneur to know these factors and get acquainted with those. More a person knows those factors better he or she will be equipped to handle those circumstances.

Factors are quite common in day-to-day life. No one can avoid this in any way. These are the part and parcel of business. Factors I am mentioning are the most common ones, but the list is endless. This depends on business to business and industry to industry. Every business and every business founder have their own price to pay. This is the fact of business. Such type of situation is faced by the business leaders quite often and quite regularly. So, these act as an important contribution of the psychological price paid.

I am here listening few factors which contributes to the psychological price. However, as I mentioned the list is endless.

I. **Pre-opening and start-up phase:** Pre-opening is the phase before the start of business. Whereas the start-up phase refers to the initial days of the business. Both the phases constitute the first steps of business. As we all know, the first step is always the toughest one. The business founder faces the maximum hurdle during these phases. These faces cover more than 50% of the difficulty. A business founder faces and deals with those. While dealing a business founder pays the psychological price. This phase is the difficult phase. A start-up founder or a business founder face various troubles in this phase. This can be in form of setup, social and personal acceptance, finance, manpower, legal matters, operational issues, sales plan EC. These factors are serious ones. So, a founder has to deal with all these. These may cause the founder stress and work overload. Founders are in extreme pressure to sort this to carry on with the business processes. This pressure is bit out of explanation for the founders. Dealing with such situation is it stressful at times.

II. **Investor handling:** Most of the business unit requires finance. This comes in form of equity or debt finance. These finances are required for setting up business facilities, manufacturing, plants and machineries, running cost of business. Handling investor is a full-time job. Connect with investor and setting the deal is the first step. This step requires a lot of workouts and discussions. Such deals are done with care, taking the note of payable and related terms. This is the process which is quite stressful. All such discussions, need to be done in very effective way. Once the deal is done keeping the investor relation is important. Investor relation is also a very sophisticated process. This too faces some type of complications during its course and tenure. These are generally sorted with discussions, but a small fraction of the cases turned ugly as well. Overall process is important, but this can lead to very stressful situations. This can lead to psychological price for start-up founders. Such psychological price takes a toll on founder and contribute to more such factors

III. **Operations and breakdown:** Operations of business is the time when a lot of issues come up. Such issues can be of high concern as it can put a stop on the regular operation of business. Apart from operational issues, the breakdown is another factor of concern. The breakdown can lead to prolonged stop of business operations. The operational issues are vital for business as it leads to disruption of manufacturing or service delivery. Operational issues can be a recurrent or non-recurrent. So, the recurrent operational issues keep appearing again and again. Non-recurrent issues are not expected to return once sorted and in short run. Every time an operational issue comes up, it hampers production - either it stops or reduces the capacity. This reduces the output and subsequently the sale and revenue. At times, breakdown is another scary affair. Breakdown is the temporary stopping of the production or service delivery for a short period or a prolonged period. This can lead to the serious consequences in business. This might require a monetary involvement as well. Both the issues are stressful in nature and leads to the psychological price speak by the founder.

IV. **Handling Co-founders:** Co-founders join business as an additional hand. They share same vision, same mindset and same goal. They take up and share the task. They help the business to achieve the goal fast. This is the positive side of having a co-founder. However, many a times the things do not go so well. That disputes between cofounder are quite normal and these are resolved by the right mechanisms in business. Issue starts appearing when one or more co-founder deviates from the path. This is a serious situation. Many business units face this situation. Disputes among co-founders can ruin a business. Handling co-founder is a very tough call. Co-founders are the part of business. So, tackling the related issues become a stressful affair. At times, negotiating issues with co-founder too becomes tough. Such situation causes a lot of stress for the business founders. Such situations can lead to many unfavourable situations. Such type of incidents is terrific for business. Founders of business invest money, time and career for business. This too gets on stake. So, it is a tremendous psychological price for a business founder.

V. **Pre-break-even time:** Breakeven is the point where the revenue just crosses the cost incurred. After this, business starts seeing profit. Just the journey before this point is quite tough. Pre breakeven phase do not bring any profit or income to the business as their revenue do not cover the costs incurred. This is a stressful situation for the business. This is quite common. Founders have financial commitments, unless the breakeven happens, one cannot fulfil those commitments. Delay in breakeven is another disturbing factor. Such delay effects the financial health of the company as well. Apart from the external factors like market demand, technical factors, government policies, too impacts the breakeven point. Without this there is no return on investment. Owners, at times, keep paying for the expenses of that phase. So, it could be another stress factor in business. This phase even sees many other problems. Founders must sort such phase and keep going. Irrespective of time taken for break events owners have to keep the show going.

VI. **Legal and compliance issues:** Legal and compliance are vital factors in business. The legal issues are always scary for the business founders. These come up because of various reasons. Sometime these come because of some shortcomings whereas sometimes it can come up due to the various external factors unrelated to business. Compliance is set of regulations which business unit has to follow as a part of business. These are times complicated set of rules. Sometimes failure to do so result in compliance related issues. Compliance related issues may lead to penalties and related actions. Such may become troublesome for business owners. Both the issues are stressful. Both the situations can lead to dangerous consequences in business. Many times, it may lead to suspension of operations. Sorting these are time taking affairs and require a lot of hard work. Such issues are very troublesome and very disheartening. These issues add to the psychological price of business for business founders. These may lead to the stress factor for business founders.

VII. **Operational issues:** Operational involves a lot of activities. Such activities may lead to the operational issues at times. Such issues are bit worrisome for founders. Such operational issues can put a halt to the production or service delivery. Stopping production can be a loss-making event for the business. Stopping operation means halting production. Such type of halt has a negative impact on revenue of business. With such impact on revenue, it is quite understood to have its impact on cash flow too. Impact on cash flow is a great concern. Operational issues also had its impact on the customer commitments. Unfulfilled customer commitment imparts negative impact on the reputation and goodwill. Such issues are too stressful to handle. Sorting such issues are tedious task. Reason for being tedious is because of operational issues. Various reasons like labour unrest, breakdown, legal issues, technical issues, low demand etc. Sorting one issue is completely different from other. Sorting these required numerous efforts. This is another factor contributing to the psychological price.

VIII. **Financial matters:** Business revolves around finance. This is the most crucial factor of business. This presents the real health of business. However, the business finance is not an easy game. This is one of the most complicated aspects. Finance is a complicated factor. Managing such factors are the key for a successful business. These factors require a lot of skill to handle. These are very high-end entrepreneur skills. Financial factors may include managing cash flow system, fundraising, managing expenses, making budgets, handling payouts, handling taxations etc. All these aspects are highly specialised ones. Such streams make the pillar of business. A business founder needs to have a grip on whole financial aspect. Such process is quite stressful. The regular follow up, monitoring and action are required. Further on audits are to be conducted on regular basis. All these processes add to the psychological price of entrepreneurship.

IX. **Setbacks on failures:** Everything cannot succeed in business. Setbacks and failures are quite common. setbacks are quite depressing. Many a times such situations lead to monetary downfall as well. These are very tough to handle at times. Founders has external financial commitment, hence the setback can impact those as well. Re-making the entire stuff while moving ahead is the most difficult part of business. It requires a lot of hard work and effort. Such efforts are stressful and time taking. Handling such situation required nerves of steel. This requires a lot of emotional control as well. Such situation even led to huge psychological price. Such price cannot be measured in numbers. For a same situation one pays higher price whereas other pays low. Such things are relative in nature. Such things are meant for strong people. Entrepreneurship has a lot of setbacks and failures. Such failures are steppingstones of success. However, converting failures to success is a very stressful job. These takes at all on start-up founders.

X. **Losses and damages:** Losses and damages are regular affairs of a business. Most of the time losses are related to monetary damages. Such type of losses is heavy on the book of accounts. Many a times, one has to take external funding to deal with such situations. So, this might cause a lot of distress. Damages can be of various types. If the business assets are damaged, re-installing those, can be a humongous effort. This also is time consuming. This event leads to collateral damage in business. Damages can lead to some additional monetary burden on business. Losses are of various types. Such type of losses not only have impact on business but also on founders. Losses are always having a negative impact on business and its reputations. Such impacts are long lasting. Many business activities like fundraising, scale up, expansion gets impacted. Many new plans get deferred. Many restructurings of business has to be done. Overall losses and damages are quite troublesome for our business founder.

XI. **Manpower related issues:** Human resources is the biggest resource. Entire business runs on this resource. Resource makes the business run. Manpower issues are quite common in business. This may be in different forms. This may be in form of high attrition rates, low productivity, indiscipline, unskilled employees, regular mistakes, union issues, strikes etc. Manpower issues are bit tricky to handle. Most of the time there is no hard and fast room for this. Every issue need to be dealt in its own way. Every lock has its own key. Manpower issues are very sensitive in nature. This has to be handled with utmost care. Many a times, negotiation has to be called for this. So, negotiation can be loss-win or win-loss but hardly win-win. Being a sensitive issue handling too requires a lot of caution. This at times, becomes stressful factor. The factor take a lot of time to solve. It might lead to interruption of operation, financial issues, losses and damages. This has a collateral impact. All these act as a factor for addition of psychological price.

XII. **Competition:** The business operates in the market with lot of competition. There are lot of players who exist in the market. Making a product rank in the market is very tough. This requires a lot of hard work and efforts. The same need to be backed by a proper planning. So, the competition is indispensable for business. The monopoly may not be the right situation now. So, handling and dealing with competition is a full-time job for a business founder. Monitoring competition is a job which starts even before the start of operations of business. Many times, competition give tough time to a business. So, condition is a factor which requires some specialised way of handling. In certain situations, competition can take certain way which may be termed as unethical. These are tough to handle under set parameters. Many a times, competition can even lead to closure of business. Right strategy for this is very important. Handling competition gives goosebumps. This event becomes quite stressful at time. One has to consider a lot of options for handling competition. Many of those work. Many do not work. This adds up to the psychological price of entrepreneurship.

XIII. **Scalability and expansion:** All businesses need to scale up. This phase is very important for growth. Scalability require a lot of planning and a lot of well-articulated actions. This takes a lot of planning. It is the most important criterion for scalability. This is a sensitive phase in business. This requires a lot of stuff and resources. These terms are very stressful at times. This forms the part of the expansion process in due course of time. Expansion is beyond scalability. This is a phase which requires full attention. Scalability is a phase which may go wrong if not planned well. Scalability phase going wrong can be a big disaster. This can really turn to be a stressful event. So, this is very delicate phase. Most of the time, this phase consumes a lot of resources. So, the phase going wrong can cost a lot a lot of monetary involvement. Scalability is dream of a every founder but going wrong can be very disheartening. This takes a lot of psychological prices. Stressful situation in this phase is quite common. Scalability must be executed with utmost care. So, this can add as a factor for psychological price for business founders.

XIV. **Sustainability:** Sustaining of business is a real skill this may refer to initial years or difficult types. Sustaining your business requires a lot of efforts. So, sustaining a business is a test of entrepreneurship. There is no hard and fast rule for this. Rather it depends on circumstances and situations. Sustaining requires a lot of on ground activities. This requires a lot of hard work. This can even go for years. Many people leave and go during this phase. Many run away and quit. Many break down. But one who continues wins !!! This is the golden rule of business. Sustaining phase may be very tough. So, when a business gets through this phase the founder may have a lot of stress. Improper handling of this phase can lead to closure of business as well. So, the fear of closure always mounts. But this most of the time opens new avenues of business. One need to have a very strong mindset to face these. Despite so much stress the end of phase brings a lot of positivity. But the phase may add as a factor in psychological price of entrepreneurship.

These factors are just a few to mention. The list can be endless. Depending on the situation and industry this varies. Many people plan this in many ways. Many got impacted and pay a lot of psychological prices. These prices are relative in nature. Some high price for the same situation as compared to others. Situation plays a vital role here. Situation is a great deciding factor. However, one must know the psychological price is indispensable for business. No one can avoid this. One has to be ready for such price. Such may be termed as one of the laws of nature. So, the price is one of the aspects of business. Without paying this price business cannot roll. So, this is one of the vital things for commencement of business. One must know that contributing factor for the price. Right assessment of these factors can be of great help.

The unspoken emotions

Human beings do have emotions. Emotions are instinct of a human being. This is a real aspect of human behaviour. So, the emotions are quite common. Like every human instinct, the founders too have emotions. But this is not the problem. The real problem comes when every emotion of a business founder remains within him or her. This is very common situation with the founder. While running a business, all the matters remain within the founder. I must say he or she can hardly share such things with his or her team. This may be in form of financial matters, funding, issues with co-founders, manpower issues, scalability issues, investor related issues etc. Under such circumstances, it is common to feel sad and depressed. But such emotions can be expressed as it might have a negative impact on team. So, the prevention of negative impact leads to suppression of emotion by the business founders. So, the emotion of a founder are always unspoken. Another reason for this is, these emotions cannot be discussed with family as well.

Such emotions impact a founder as a person or a human being. So, such emotions remain as a suppressed factor inside the founder. Such emotions are very personal at times. Such emotions do require a place to be spoken or discussed. But most of the corners, this cannot be done. So, these are real stuffs. These might be a great source of psychological distress. Such type of distress takes a lot of time to get repaired. Unspoken emotion is one of the key factors of founder's distress. Emotions are the natural instincts of a person. Hence same is the case with business founders. Unspoken emotions may not be counted as one of the direct reasons for distress. Instead can act as one of the contributing factors of psychological price. Unspoken emotion may or may not cause any issue in short run but rather it's effects appear in long run. So, the issue appears days, months or years later. But this might impact the founder in some cases the business units too.

Ways to negotiate psychological price

Every founder pays psychological price for business. Some pays higher price pays a lower price. But the price is paid for sure. There are many ways by which one can negotiate these psychological price contributors. These ways are to be decided by the founders themselves. Entrepreneurship is not a profession; it is a life itself. So, one must modify lifestyle in order to get the psychological price negotiated.

I am mentioning here few points for negotiating psychological price.

i. **Planning:** Planning is indispensable virtue in business. The business cannot go without this. Planning is one way using with the psychological price can be negotiated. One must first plan the business. Remember planning must be on pen and paper. So, this is a great step. Planning can lead to step-wise and phase-wise procedural description. This is of great help to the business founders. Planning sets the workflow as well. This keeps a business affair as per laid the steps and related efforts. Also, required resources allocation is also presented in this phase. The planning helps to keep the things in order as far as possible. Moreover, it leads to organised work. Organised work helps to counter many starting hassles. This takes up a huge amount of stress from founders. At the same time, it is important tool to measure and define the yardstick of progress. Every detail in project has to be noted, in advance by making and following the plan. This helps to initiate necessary corrective action on time. Most of the time such corrective actions can help to overcome the hassles related to the project. This can be a great preventive tool for entrepreneurs. This can act as the great blessing. Planning has a lot of collateral benefits in business. It streamlines work and aids in regular monitoring. Such processes are great tools to check the mistakes and prevent deviations. The prevention of deviation can keep the business on track. Overall planning, help to keep the psychological price on check by organised work. Regular check and timely preventive actions

ii. **Prototype and process recce:** Prototype is the first show or make of the product or service model. This is a miniature version of the whole business. This is the time wherein one makes the first show. Most of the time, this is done for a review. Many stakeholders, both internal and external review that. This review gives a lot of feedback - both positive and negative. With feedback, one can have a huge way for improvement. This helps to overcome many initial defects and shortcomings. This helps a founder to pinpoint the issues and take corrective measures. Such measures help to minimise the losses and blunders. This saves a business from disruptions and hassles. One must be very serious with the prototype making. Feedbacks are very vital. It is equally important to act on the feedbacks received. Such feedback and collaborative actions are very crucial. Apart from prototype, process are also run on trial basis. The pros and cons of processors are noted, and corrective action is taken. This saves a business from business issues.

iii. **Mindset:** Mindset of a business founder is very important. A founder must have very strong and positive mindset. Mindset of a founder plays an important role. Founders with positive mindset pay less psychological price for business and vice versa. Mindset is a key factor in dealing with the situation. Mindset is a great tool for a business founder. So, the mindset need to be under control and positive for a business founder. Good mindset helps a founder to make better decisions and face difficult situations in a well organised manner. How can one make the mindset right and positive? There is no hard and fast rule for this. Rather this depends on the situation to situation. This might include walk around woods, meditating, reading good books, listening to motivating podcast, watching inspirational videos etc. All these are trusted and age-old exercises to keep good and healthy mindset. Even many subconscious exercises too play a great role. This might include repeating an affirmation, imaging a great and positive scene etc. These exercises have great impact on brain. In fact, these affects sub-conscious part of brain in a positive way. Yoga too plays a vital role. These all have an impact in long run. This rectifies a wrong mindset, which in turn, helps to face ups and downs of business in a better way. Such positive mindset leads to low psychological price of business.

iv. **Lifestyle modification:** Psychological price of entrepreneurship leads to a lot of health hazards and lifestyle ailments. So, the best way to reduce the impact is by throwing lifestyle modifications. This has many positive impacts in personal and professional life. Lifestyle modification can be in many ways. This can happen by taking up exercise, waking up in the morning, eating healthy etc. These all help a lot to overcome the lifestyle disorders to a huge extent. By doing so, lifestyle disorder can get reduced and subsequently psychological price too gets reduced. Lifestyle modification is also good for one's own health, mind and body. In fact, this keeps the doctor away. In today's lifestyle, diseases are quite common. Every household has at least one person with such diseases. Unhealthy lifestyle is the key contributor for this. Such modifications keep the mind and body fresh. It helps to face any difficult situations in business. Lifestyle modifications also include keeping a proper sleep cycle. This helps in treating the fatigue as well. This is required to keep the health in a proper way. Keeping lifestyle disorders away is also a moto. Lifestyle modification has also a positive impact on mental health. This in turn, creates many positive impacts on business founder. Positive mentality helps in good decision making and facing a tough time. In the face of distress, disciplined lifestyle prevents the breakdown and the ailments. Lifestyle helps to be in good mental and physical health for a longer duration. With good mental and physical health, psychological price of entrepreneurship to gets reduced.

v. **Mentorship:** I have already mentioned that time and again that mentorship is a vital factor in business. Mentors are very experienced people in business. They have lots of experience. A mentee, really benefit from experience of a mentor. Mentorship has got many benefits. Such benefits might come up in form of handholding strategy, guiding and walking through as well. Mentorship not only helps to keep the journey proper, rather it helps to avoid the pitfalls as well. This saves a founder from various issues and probable problems. Such type of hand holding is boon for business. This prevents many losses and mistakes. Hence, helps a founder in big way. Hence, his or her stress factor too gets low. This further leads to lower psychological price. Mentorship comes at various levels. This takes from pre-launch level to going till IPO and even after that. Mentorship is another way to reach the goal fast and in proper and organised way. So have a mentor and look for a well-organised entrepreneurship journey.

vi. **External help:** Many times, business founder has to take external help to deal with a situation. There nothing wrong with it. Many big firms hire professional consultants for this job. External help comes with various set of skills and expertise. One has to pinpoint the skill and expertise required to sort a situation. This comes with a cost. Such external helps may ask for a fee in lieu of their service. So before selecting an external help or consultation one must be clear with the type of the service required. In order to do that, one has to first pinpoint the problem areas. Defining the problem is not an easy task. This requires a thorough analysis. Such analysis is very important for determination of the consultancy. This comes in form of financial, operational, sales, legal etc. So based on the problem faced, one has to opt for the consultancy type. Right selection can lead to great results and vice versa. At the same time, once the external help is decided and contracted, the plan for the execution must be in place. This must be initiated properly in a well-planned manner. Right help is required in order to optimise the gain from the consultancy. Here, the clarity on deliverables is an important factor for both the parties. Next important factor is the time frame. External help or consultancy comes with the contracted time frame. This must be well negotiated and must be mutually agreed. I always suggest to breakdown the big task to numerous small tasks and attach a time frame to each small tasks. So, this will make the tasks well organised and with optimum monitoring opportunities. This will further help to get good results. In case of any lacking, it can be detected well in advance. This gives a lot of opportunities for timely rectification. External help is a paid service, which one need to take on periodic basis. This is a great relief for the founder for complicated issues. External help can even bring many of the new ideas. So, best part is to have a well-defined problem and take help of a well-planned external help. This reliefs a founder from sorting all issues himself or herself.

vii. **Knowing steps and processes well:** This is important for a founder to know the steps of business and processes. This helps to get acquainted with the journey. This helps to plan these things well and organise the actions in the proper way. A founder must plan well for knowing the entire process and procedure of business. Knowing this requires a lot of study, on hand experience, mentorship and planning. So, this must be thoroughly done, before the start of business. So, the process of gaining the knowledge about the various processes of business must be initiated before the start of business. Rather I must say before the planning of business. Such type of knowledge also helps to plan the steps of business. If the founder is aware of processes, he is also aware of hassles and hazards of the process. This makes them ready for issues related to those processes. Hence, one can remain prepared and plan to face those. Many times, with the right knowledge one can prevent the issues. This can be a boon for business. Prevention of occurrence of problem is one of the finest strategies. This saves a business from many unknown pitfalls. Knowing process also makes running a business smooth. No one can give you a wrong idea or suggestion if you are aware of the things. This again saves a lot of negative impacts. This is important. At the same time, knowing the things relieves mental pressure from the founder's mind. This relief can be of great help, this further lowers down the psychological price. This event saves the time of the founder for other important tasks. This further helps to prevent breakages and breakdowns to a great extent.

viii. **Analysing risk:** The risk is a common term in business. Risk is one of the inevitable factors for business. No business can run without risk being taken. Risk taking is one of the initiating points of business. This is one factor which every founder must consider. Risk brings many untoward situations too. This can be a great cause of stress. So being a founder one has to analyse and research the risks. Risks varies from business to business and industry to industry. So before starting, a founder has to first understand the risks involved in business. Risks can be of various types. This may be in form of financial risks, competition risk, compliance risk, market risk etc. All these risks and additional risks must be well assessed by the founders. This helps to get ready for facing risks. Many a times knowing risk can save or business from falling apart. Analysing must be done on pen and paper. This must be analysed on phase-wise manner because every phase of business has its own challenge. Pre-opening phase has a separate set of risks as compared to operating phase. At the same time, expansion phase has a different set of risks involved. All these are quite different from each other. Such risks need to be analysed separately and dealt in completely different way. Along with identifying risks three more points must be worked upon. First, symptoms of approach of the risk. Second, ways to prevent. Thirdly, to deal with it. Firstly, the symptoms. Before onset of risk situations many triggering factors appear. Most of the time people ignore those. This leads to fall into the risk trap. Identification of onset symptoms gives time to prepare for risk. Secondly, the ways to prevent. When you know the probable risk, you can plan for the prevention of the risks. This helps a lot. Many a times, this helps in preventing the impact of risk. So, remember prevention is better than cure. Thirdly the ways to deal with it. At times, in spite of so many preventive measures, a risky situation cannot be avoided. Here comes one must plan for ways to deal with it. This must be well planned from before. Also, necessary resources must be allocated for facing those. This planning prevents many interruptions and obstructions to operations. All types of businesses, irrespective of big and small have to prepare for facing risks. Big companies can always be better prepared as compared to smaller ones as they have got huge resources allocated for this. Smaller companies might face issues in this, due to the lesser resources they have. But it is important for both type of companies to analyse and get prepared for the risks.

ix. **Incubation:** Incubation offers a complete ecosystem for initial phase of business. I wrote a full chapter on this already. Incubation offers many benefits like full support, mentorship, networking opportunities, office space etc. This is really a boon for new businesses. Apart from this, offers a business founder or support during initial days of business. Initial days of business are quite tough in nature. This makes the wave for foundation of business. Such incubation centres are of great help and assistance. Best part of it is, guidance which a start-up company gets. Guidance is of great help for businesses. Incubation acts as a system of hand holding. This handholding relieves the business founder from most of the worries. This is not only relieving from worries but also helps to overcome many other hassles as well. Incubation provides a business a well-organised framework for business. So, this is a great concept to know and lowers down the psychological price of business.

x. **Delegation:** Delegation is one of the indispensable factors for business. A founder cannot do all the work alone. He always requires a team. Once he has got a team, he needs to delegate the tasks to the team. Delegation is a vital phenomenon. Right delegation is the key for an effective business operation. Delegation must be done properly. That too in a well organised manner. Delegation must be carried with the ownership and regular monitoring. This is important. Delegation helps to overcome the excess workload from the founder. This helps in agility and taking more tasks at a time. This helps in maintaining the efficiency of business operations. With this, chances of mistake to gets down. With more efficiency, more work can be done in the lesser unit of time. This helps a business to earn more revenue. Many founders are reluctant in team formation, which is the basic requirement for delegation. This might be because of the fixed cost which comes up during the phase. Now a days, outsourcing too can help in delegation of work. This can be explored on the case-to-case basis, rather than a fixed cost unlike the team formation. This is even good for smaller businesses. Even freelancers can be helpful. This offers quality work at a reasonable price. Delegation is the key for all types of business scale-up. One person cannot do all work himself or herself. This is one of the key elements. This relieves a founder in a big way. At the same time, it reduces the psychological price of entrepreneurship.

xi. **Structured organisational layout:** In order to have the delegation factor work well, organizational structure of the company has to be defined well. A well-defined organization layout is very important. This creates a good company governance. A structured organization and the well layout are the secret for this. This helps in organised work and leads to a lot of related advantages. This helps to organise the flow of communication and the right flow of instructions. This also minimises the issues and disputes. This further helps to keep the cost under control. Structured aspect makes the team, clear with their job roles and reporting structures. This reporting structure is very important in an organization. This makes the flow of instruction and feedback in a well channelized way. This further makes managing the human resources better. Once again to say, human resources is the most complicated resource in business. This relieves a founder from the issues related to this sophisticated resource. This can be a big relief. This lowers the psychological price for the founder.

xii. **Company governance:** Company governance is one of the most important aspects of business. This defines the role and power of the stakeholders. This differentiates the role along with the definition required for a well organization for business. This prevents excessive intervention or responsibility avoidance by the stakeholders. Both the situations are quite disaster us for business. Company governance is also liked by investors and lenders. The investor will like a company which has a well-defined governance in place. On the other hand, if the governance is not in place it might lead to a lot of conflicts, disputes, and too much intervention by certain stakeholders. These are very boring situations for a business. This creates a lot of stress for a business founder. Solving these problems are big hassles and take a lot of time and energy. This is stressful also. So, the proper company governance solves this issue to a huge extent. So, this further reliefs a founder from such hassles. Many people say company governance is for large companies. But this is a myth. All companies need this. A founder must draft this before the start of the company.

xiii. **Organizational SOP:** Here SOP refers to standard operating procedures. The standard procedures are very important for operational part of a company. SOP helps to maintain quality and efficiency of operation. This might seem like a complicated matter initially. But it gives a great result in long run. This also minimises the chances of accidents. This prevents wastages and pilferage is also. Operational SoP acts as a guidance for operation. Such guidance, must be followed. These checks the deviation as well. This helps to streamline the process of operations. Such streamlined business processes are blessing for business. This solves majority of problems. Even the small companies must set operational SOPs. This is appreciated for all businesses and of all scale. The operational SOP can be a great relief for the founder. This relieves founders from most of the stress due to operational issues.

xiv. **Insuring:** There are many factors which are beyond control of anyone. Business faces a lot of contingency as well. Insurance is a great way to deal with it. Insurance must be selected with proper care and the right consultation. Insurances come with various types of covers. This might be in form of fire and peril insurance, liability insurance, officers insurance etc. Business founder has to access the risk first, then only one can look for adequate cover. This must be done with care and with right consultation. Improper insurance will not serve any purpose. At the same time, over insuring can be an unwanted expense. Under insurance might provide inadequate coverage. Business faces contingencies day in and day out. Such contingency creates a lot of stress for a business founder. This might be a very tough call at times. This is mainly because such issues are beyond control. This insurance can act as a great relief.

xv. **Creating social circle:** Social circle is a great option. In fact, socialization is an art. This creates a lot of impact for business. Social circle can be in form of business option or organization. There are many organizations which aid in making social cum business circle. This can be of great help in case of referral or assistance. It is said that network is the net worth. Social networking can make a great and positive impression. Referrals for business as well as cross referral can be generated. Such referrals can act as a great source of business. There are organizations like BNI, which acts as great source of referral. This helps in knowing about a lot of factors which affects business. This helps in knowing the business environment in a better way. Knowing those are the real blessings for business. Many a times, social circle helps in adverse situation. This makes a lot of impact and assists in helping to overcome many adverse situations. This relieves a founder from stress to a huge extent.

xvi. **Place to Discuss problems:** The business, just like any other work, has a problem on and off. It is important for a business founder to have a place to say and discuss the business problems. It can be different for different people. This could be a friend, a mentor, a co-founder or anyone of trust. This may be a professional place or a personal in nature. Here the trust is a real factor one must look for. The person with whom you are looking to share the problem should keep those facts with him or her only. He or she must not share these with anyone. This relieves a founder psychologically from a lot of stress. Most of the time one can even get the right advisory. This can be a great option. Please to discuss can be a great way to relieve oneself from stress of the situation. One must not disclose each and everything during the process. Vital information must not be disclosed under any circumstances. This can be a great stress relieving method for a business founder.

xvii. **Cut off from negativity:** Negativity is everywhere. It is widespread in televisions, news, social media, messaging apps etc. All these creates an aura of negativity. Negative interpretation of a fact too creates a lot of negative environments. Unfiltered social media is further adding fuel to the fire. It has its impact on human mind. This makes one's thinking negative. It creates demotivation and makes depressing environment. All these are very harmful for our mental health. This in turn has an impact on work and business. This further creates an atmosphere of fear and rejection. As a founder, one has to understand that the negativity is normal part of life. Hence, at times, cutting off from the negativity must be planned. One must not consume negative stuffs on regular basis. Creating a negativity barrier is very important for the business owners. Negative auras need to be cleared, under all circumstances. This restores confidence and improves work quality of business. Further it relieves a founder from unnecessary thoughts and stress.

xviii. **Close circle discussion:** It is always recommended that a closed circle be made for important discussions. This close circle can be the confidants of founders. This may be in form of co-founder, team members, close friends, mentors etc. This circle can be a great space for business. A founder can discuss a lot of things about business with this circle which cannot be discussed in open forums. This can even help to strategize the business. Close circle helps to keep the strategy confidential and with right people. Close circle helps a business founder to discuss many business and related issues. This can relieve a business founder from many stressful aspects of business. The business gets into many phases - easy and tough; profit and loss; upward and downward etc. Such phases are having issues of their own. Hence, these issues can be well described with this circle. Many times, it acts as a place for just sharing the experiences. Just sharing the stuff, can be a great psychological relief for a founder.

xix. **Ignoring the crowd:** Crowd mentality is very complicated. This follows the trend which goes from ages. Anything new is not liked by the crowd. So, whatever a business founder does may or may not be liked by the crowd. The result of this – criticism, bullying, backbiting and discouragement. These things are quite common. Most of the business founders face those. These puts a negative impact on founder. There is no hard and fast rule to prevent or cure this. Best way to deal with this is, to ignore the crowd and remain focus on your purpose. This might not be easy, at times, as the crowd form the environment nearby. But regular practice of ignoring the negative crowd helps. Also, keep avoiding negative people, negative discussions and negative environment as well. So, turning the eye away from such element can help to cut off from the negative factor. This is a great relieving factor. This relieves a lot of unnecessary stress from a person.

xx. **Self-development schedule:** Self-development is a great module. Many people avoid this, Stating the self-development might not be required for them. Many consider this as an unnecessary time and resource utilization. However, self-development module is much more than that. This helps to manage oneself in a better way especially in the difficult situations. This helps to manage the emotion in a better way for self-development. It helps in uplifting of one's personality. In today's world self-development helps a person in many situations of life. This can even manage stressful situations in life. The self-development relieves a lot of stress. Self-help modules can be a blessing for a start-up founder. Such start-ups and their founder will have a better purview of the issues and the better way of handling those. This relieves a founder from excessive stress or related issues. This reduces the psychological price to a huge extent.

Psychological price is inevitable and indispensable. No one can avoid this. But what a founder can do, is it can make a better way to deal with those. One must not get scared with this. One has to understand that these factors are regular affairs of business. Better handling the situation is the key for this.

Most of the people are not aware of the psychological price one has to pay for entrepreneurship. Without knowing, if such situation appears, the founder is not well prepared. This makes them totally unprepared for forthcoming events. This results in wrong decisions, losses, hassles, penalties, stress, breakdowns etc. All these can be easily avoided with the right planning and well organised actions. Moreover, positive mindset plays a big role. Psychological price can be bad for a founder. One need to handle this properly in a right way.

CHAPTER XI

Nurturing The Mind

Mind is a great instrument. It has got amazing powers. This is amazing piece of instrument ever created on this planet. It has power to do amazing work. Many famous & successful personalities have nurtured the power of this, to get the great works done. Nothing can beat this.

It is said that what we use, is just a fraction of our mind and rest remains under-utilised or unutilised. So, this is a great option for doing great things. The ancient Indian sages have advocated various techniques for this. They did a lot of mental exercises to explore the hidden power of the mind. Ancient Indian texts too mentioned a lot about this.

Many artists, creators, musicians, writers, leaders, inventors have used and made their work in mind before making it a reality. There are numerous examples of this. This can offer a lot of scope for business founders to beat their fear, using the mind nurturing techniques.

The creation space for fear and phobia is mind. All emotions are the first generated in minds then expressed. Same is true in case of fear. Mind with its thoughts creates fear. Then it gets expressed in form of actions, words and expressions. This makes the way for rest of the actions related to fear.

My idea of stressing the mind and its matter, is to fight the fear in organised way. If the mind is well conditioned, the fear generation processes can be greatly reduced. Even if it is created, it can be well handled. This will help a business founder to keep the work aligned with the goal. Mind can even help a founder to face a situation in a better way. This eases out the situation for the founder. This can even uplift the mood of the founders. This makes the mindset positive and motivated.

Mind can be positive or negative

As I mentioned mind can either be positive or negative. **Whatever mind absorbs it reflects that.** So, if the mind absorbed positive stuffs, it reflects positive and vice versa. Mind reflects the absorbed matter. So, the stuff which mind absorbs, makes it either positive or negative.

Mind can make the environment likewise. Positive mind can make the environment positive and vice versa. A positive mind is an optimistic mind. This can handle the situation in an effective and efficient way. This can leave an unexplored opportunity in a difficult situation. This can even reduce the stress of a founder. Further on, business issues can be well handled in a positive situation. So, a positive situation is a blessing. This blessing is cultivated by a positive mind only.

On contrary, a negative mind makes the environment negative. This negativity is quite troublesome for business. This can even make the simple situations complicated. A negative mind can even miss the new opportunities in business. A negative mind will find it tough to handle a situation. Improper handling can even destroy the business to a great extent.

One has to choose the difference between both.

Positive mind	Negative mind
Handles situation well	Mishandles situation
Faces problems well	Faces problems improperly
Managers problems	Mismanages problems
Sees opportunities	Misses opportunities
Relieves stress	Creates stress
Create a good environment	Creates a poor environment
Motivates co-workers	Demotivates Co workers

Pic 1

We can find both type of people in business. The negative people will have tough time in dealing with the situation. On contrary, this can even be a better walk for the positive minded people. So, the positive people will always have an edge over the negative people. So, this factor has a lot of impact on the business founders. Positive minded people have a lower fear factor as compared to the negative minded people.

Negativity: A magnet

Negativity is an amazing magnet. It sticks a mind to it, for a long time. The people get attracted to negativity soon and easily. This is everywhere now. It is in news channels, in social media, in talks in discussions etc. All these contents have a lot of capacity to make a person glue to it for hours.

Negativity or negative content attracts a lot of people. This works like a magnet. So, this attracts a lot of crowds. So, this makes the news channels, media social, print medias and messaging apps stick to these. More these exercises go on as more crowds it attracts. Human mind is an unfiltered one and which likes the negative stuff to a huge extent.

Another aspect of negativity is interpretation. Content can be interpreted either in the positive way or in negative way. Interpretation can make a lot of impact – both positive & negative. Even the positive steps can be interpreted in a negative way or vice versa. This interpretation fascinates the audience. Most of the people like to hear about the interpretation of happening rather than the happening. Various forms of media describe and interpretate the same thing in different ways. Here, comes the importance of interpretation. Most ironical part is during interpretation certain points are stressed and certain points are left. So, the preference of content lies with the person writing the interpretation. This creates either positive or negative contents. Neutral interpretation is rare. In neutral interpretation the mention of positive and negative points will have same weightage. Such neutral interpretation leaves the decision on the audience to appreciate or criticise any scenario.

As a human being not getting attracted to negative stuff is quite difficult. This requires an effort of conscious brain. This requires filtering the receipt of the information inflow. Second thing is a voiding the interpretation. One must make the repeated efforts to get away from the magnetic effects of negativity.

<u>Positivity - A tough terrain</u>

Positivity is rare nowadays. One has to search for it using microscope. Even the positive effects are presented in a negative way now a days. This further makes the mind and environment negative. The part of positivity is not easy. First of all, the positive contents are tough to find. One has to find and analyse it well. Then only, they can realise the impacts as positive. Finding such content itself takes a lot of time and effort. Many a times, interpretation makes a positive impact, a negative one.

Same is the situation for business founders. At the start of the business, or at the time of planning mostly the negative stuff only gets projected. This happens by known people. The good or successful step is shown as a difficult terrain. The steps to those are shown in a very tough and hard to travel way. This creates a lot of discouragement for new business founders. Such discouragement creates a lot of psychological stress as well. Showing success as a tough journey is another example of interpretation.

Such success requires a lot of hard work. This is true for all walks of life including business. No stream of walk is a cakewalk. This is a great stuff and fact. Seem is the fact for business. This requires a lot of efforts. This is not only the case for business.

So, projecting a positive impact with tough road projection is partially right. Every good result requires prolonged preparation and hard work. At the same time, it is not a route to hell. Every successful people walk on this road. For a business, success of founder to have to walk the tough walk. It is important for a founder to see their journey as a positive, one not as a tough terrain. This positive thought will be of great help to the founders. So, whenever a journey of entrepreneurship start, it goes through the difficulties and hardships. This is normal and expected.

Negativity - A reason of stop

Flow of negativity is the real reason for discouragement for many works including business. Flow of negativity put a new work in poor light. This makes the mind totally negative. This acts as a big-time hindrance and discouragement. So, this can be a vital reason.

Discouragement flows in from the sources of negativity. Negative makes the mind confused and fearful. This further weakens the confidence of a person. In day to day life such negativity flows in from various sources like friends, families, colleagues, media, social media etc. Such contents, news, advises and unsolicited opinions have got deep impact on one's thinking - mostly negative. Such negative impact results in negative aura and environment. Such an environment does not lead to any good stuff.

As we all know, for all type of work or the job, right and positive mindset is essential factor. This factor is a great spoil spot for all type of activities. The negative thinking really stops the start of every type of work to the fullest. So, the factor is strong break for all.

In case of business, it is quite easy to project the negative aspect, as the journey is full of hardship ups and downs. One just need to clarify the down aspect of entrepreneurship. In order to make it a negative trend. So, this is the aspect which can take easy turn towards negativity. This has the capacity to discourage people from getting into it. In other words, it puts a full stop. This is a regular affair for entrepreneurs' journey.

This cycle of negativity and discouragement goes on. This is a cycle which keeps rolling unchecked. This unchecked roll, effects many minds and thought processes. So, this makes the environment negative and discouraging. This is also supported by the people who had a setback in the journey of entrepreneurship. That too clarifies the negative aspects of business. So, the way the negative things are circulated, and the negative things are well projected in certain interpreted way. The interpretation further complicates the matter. Such aspects are too difficult to assess or counter.

Mindset a solution

Best way to fight negativity is the mindset. Mindset has amazing power to sort their thoughts and form a positive trend. Mindset can act as a weapon to sort the issues related to this. Mindset which is positive can do a lot of good and efficient work. At the same time, a negative mindset can create a lot of hindrances. This prevents a person from taking up any new project and deals. This is a great concern.

Next the solution part of it is to make the mindset right for work. The work of the mindset makes the impact in a big way. This show of impact may take a little time. This is the phase when one start losing the patience. This makes the way for the path to take tough decisions.

The right mindset is a blessing for a business founder. Right mindset makes that difficult situations favourable. So, this can be of great help. This makes the way for great achievement in long run. This facilitates good decision making and wonderful work environment. This leads to the work and right thoughts. The challenge here is creating a right mindset. This is a great way to deal with the situation. But the problem is, environment around us are so negative that it is tough to make the mindset positive. One has to fight a lot to keep the mind on positive note. A lot of conscious exercise is required for this.

Following are some of the exercise which can help you on this.

i. **Filter the information inflow:** It is important to check the flow of information into the brain. One need to filter the negative info and allow the positive ones.

ii. **Cut off from the negativity:** Cut the negative sources of information. Cutting off the negativity is one of the best solutions of mindset handling.

iii. **Get into positive stuff:** Positive stuff has an amazing power. So, a business founder has to follow the positive content to keep the mindset positive.

iv. **Focus on set goals:** Being a business founder, it is important to have a goal set. Once the goal is set, the founder must focus on that only. Focus on the goal keeps the momentum on and the mindset engaged in work. And engaged mindset has no room for negativity.

Subconscious an unexplored territory

It is said that we use just a part of our brain. Most part of the brain remain unused. This is a fact which, opens a lot of avenues for improvement. Many ancient Indian sages advocated many techniques and arguments for use of the brain to the fullest. This can be of great help for business founders.

Subconscious is that part of the brain which is not directly controlled by us. This is the part which is not explored by most of the people. Subconscious mind is a powerful tool. The power of subconscious mind is well described by Dr Joesph Murphy In his book "The Power Of Your Sub-Conscious Mind". This book mentions some of the amazing techniques for using and harnessing the power.

Subconscious mind can be of great help for business founders, so the founders have to be well aware of the importance of this. Many of the situations which a founder faces, can be handled well with involvement of subconscious mind. This plays a role - both in form of positive and negative. So, it is important to seek the positive role from the subconscious mind on this. There are many ways you can explore and nurture the subconscious mind to your benefit. Ancient Indian sages suggested many such techniques in ancient texts. Apart from the ancient texts, modern science too suggest many such techniques.

I am suggesting the following points

i. **Repetitions**: Repetitions of certain positive statements on regular basis has a lot of positive impact on subconscious. The founder can even repeat their mission statement, goals or target plans. Repetitions on regular basis can help one's brain and thought processes sync with the goal and mission. Ancient Indian text termed this process as *"japa'*. In ancient India, sages used to do *"japa"* and repeat the names of the God or religious texts. This used to stick their mind to phrase. This subconscious nurturing technique works in an amazing way

ii. **Imagination**: One has to use the technique of imagination to create the environment targeting. This process is widely used by artists. They imagine their artwork before getting it created.

iii. **Meditating on problem**: Meditation is a great process. Whenever there is an issue, it must be meditated in upon. The process focuses the whole and sole of mental energy on the issue. Our mind is an amazing machine. It has capacity to find the way. Many leaders put this technique to effect for problem solving.

Subconscious mind is a powerhouse. This is not well explored by people. So, this can be the key in dealing with the issues of entrepreneurship. This can be a great help for all type of stress related issues. This can be of help to founder, to sort many issues with deep thinking. This type of mental exercise help to keep the mind calm, composed and focused. These elements are real blessing in the journey of entrepreneurship. So, nurturing the subconscious mind can lead to a lot of benefits in long run.

So, managing such situations with the right mindset is the key. Right use of subconscious mind can be of great help

Find ikigai

Ikigai is a Japanese term which means "purpose to be". This is the term which is of utmost importance for a business founder. Before start, a founder has to find his or her ikigai. Finding ikigai is crucial, as one has to find the passion. Fighting this is required as this will help to find the founders real interest level. This makes one attached to the purpose to the soul.

Ikigai is one of the key elements for any work. If the soul and the purpose of work are not In sync, then the action does not make well. Finding ikigai makes the work and journey interesting.

Finding the purpose of life is a serious thing. One need to do a lot of brainstorming for this. So, the entrepreneur needs to do a lot of mental exercise to find the ikigai. Ikigai makes the purpose of life in sync with the business mission and vision. So even if it is found as complicated, entrepreneurs and start-up founders must go for this exercise.

I am not going deep into the concept. Rather I am making it easy to execute and understand. I am making it easy with few simple questions.

i. **What is the purpose?** Before start-up business, one need to find the purpose of starting. What exactly is the reason for business. The purpose of start, has to be well defined. A well-defined purpose of business keeps the thoughts and ideas clear and organised. Well organised idea is required to run the business well. Founder has to do a deep thinking for the purpose of business. The business which runs with well-defined purpose flourishes well. Clarity with the founder runs down to the hierarchy. Few simple points can help.

- What is founder's passion?
- What passion matches with business mission?

- What is the purpose of business?
- Who does the business benefit?
- How many lives it impacts?
- Does the expertise run with the purpose?
- Does the founder's purpose of life is In sync with the business?
- How is the business fulfilling the purpose of life?

These questions might seem easy but these required deep thinking

i. **Why should one start**? Making a head start is important. At the same time, it is important to know and find out why should one start. The reason for starting a business is quite important to understand. Many a times, founders are unclear about that. So, they are unclear about the motive. This motive becomes a tripping force for entrepreneurship journey. The reason for starting business requires a lot of introspection. This requires deep soul-steering reason. This is a great exercise. One can rediscover oneself with this. Best way to do so is by doing the following easy exercise

- Sit in a calm and quiet place.
- Take a pen and paper.
- Getaway from distractions.
- Ask yourself the reason for starting a venture.
- Note down all the point that comes in the mind - do not filter.
- Once all thoughts are noted, go through all the points and write sub points.
- Write quick narration against all the sub points.
- Run through and work on all points.
- Keep repeating unless the stuff becomes clearer.
- Relate and take it on a separate sheet of paper.

These 10 points might sound simple but requires deep thinking and mental clarity.

iii. **Will this serve my goal?** Every person in this world has some goal. Business is the means to achieve that goal. This is the cause which drives a person. So, it is important to find the work which one is starting, is able to serve the goal or not. For this exercise, it is important to find the goal first. A majority of people in the world are not aware of their goal. Without a goal the aim of life becomes totally diluted. The conviction goes missing. So, the goal identification is very important. It is completely different from the next step of professional carrier.

Let me explain this with an example

- Eyeing to become the HOD, is the next step of professional career
- Serving people by supplying easy access to medicine is the goal of life

These two have huge differences. Next is professional step is of a short-term aim. But once it become a goal can be a lifetime ambition. So before starting a business, one has to find whether it is serving the goal or not. Here, saying yes or no is not an easy task. This takes a lot of introspection and deep thought. This makes the way for finding the driving force. So, you have to make sure that venture you are making, is aligned with the whole of your life. If required, goal and business module must be modified to get the alignment right

iv. **Does this suit me?** Every person's personality is different. This makes the way for suitability of work. I cannot do all work similarly every person on this earth cannot do all work. So, it is important to find the suitability factor of the work. Suitability factor is important part of personality. This makes the way for the work done in a passionate way. This is one of the ways to self-assessment before start. The assessment requires a lot of psychometric factors. This is including personality, academics and physical factors too. There are few factors that I am mentioning which determines the suitability

a. **Mindset:** Mindset is an important factor for starting any venture. Mindset must be In sync with the venture and related requirement. Right mindset of founder is the key. The mindset makes the way for a future decision of the company. The mindset is the first factor to consider in the journey of entrepreneurship. This need to be nurtured first.

b. **Interest:** Interest is an emotional puller. This pulls the people to a new work or assignment. It is said that a person can do a job in the passionate way, in which he or she has an interest. Forcefully making people do work results in low quality work, dropouts, and psychological stress. People even get into work in which he or she is not interested. In the journey of entrepreneurship interest can be a great deciding factor. This factor can be of great influence. Without interest work can be tough to digest. In entrepreneurship journey, it is important to first find the interest. Then plan for it. This helps to have a great enjoyable journey in long run. This has a psychological impact. Interest determines whether a work or assignment is suitable for a person or not. So, this is easy to determine and explore. Interest also creates a passion for work. This is another great factor for this. Interest contributes to many direct and indirect factors. Suitability factor has a huge impact from the interest one is having. If one is given engineering-based work, but the persons interest is towards consultancy, then obviously he or she will have a stressful event. Similarly, if one has interest towards tax consultancy but given work on content making the person is bound to suffer psychologically. This is a common human factor cum behaviour. Hence the interest factor makes a lot of influence on suitability factor.

c. **Academics:** There are certain work which require an academic requirement. Some to name are medical work, legal work, auditing work et These type of require a stream of education to perform the task. These are bound by laws of the land. In such type of work, academic requirement comes first then other factors. For example, if one want to work heart surgery he or she need to be a qualified doctor. One cannot perform any treatment or surgery without proper academic qualification, even if he or she has an interest. These streams of work are sophisticated and require precision. Here the mistake is not a mistake it could be a life-threatening blunder. So, a person needs to be trained for years and years before taking up the work. So, these streams of work require academic degree to become suitable. These are different set of assignments wherein the suitability factor is determined with academic degree.

d. **Physical status:** There are certain work and assignment which require certain degree of physical health and fitness requirement. These can be specific to those type of work. For example, for being a pilot you require good eyesight. For taking up sports and related assignments certain physical health requirement are necessary. In such type of work physical health standards are of prime importance.

One cannot take up those work unless they qualify for the physical health requirements. This adds up to suitability factor for such kind of work. Even if the interest and other factors are there, the physical health can become a deciding factor. So, this deciding factor, at times make great impact. This is one of the ways, to make and determine the suitability for work. So, this factor becomes a vital one at certain work.

e. **Skill set:** Every work requires a certain type of skill set. Skill is required to perform any kind of work. Every set of work requires certain type of skill. Nowadays skill is given more relevance and place above academics in many types of assignments. So, each work stresses on the certain type of skill which are required for execution of that work. So, the check of required skill set is important before taking up any assignment. Improper skill can spoil the work and even degrade the quality of results. So the right match can be the great factor for smooth running of work. It also enhances the efficiency and quality of work. It is important to first define the skill set required. Then the right analysis of this can be an effective way of matching that.

f. **Passion:** Passion of a person is a deep emotional factor. This acts as deep connect with work. This deep connect takes the way forward for work. If the work goes well as per the passion, then the work goes fine and vice versa. First thing, one need to do is to find the passion. That is, what type of word draws the inner soul? This requires a lot of mental brainstorming. This brainstorming requires further workout as well. Passion and profession need to be In Sync. This sync is very vital. The sink can help a person to take the stuff further in a passionate way. If the passion is in order, it has to go a long way in organised work. So, passion is an emotional force for tracking the work to the next level, with a strong emotional connect.

Ikigai A force

Ikigai is a great force for businesspersons. This force helps to take many steps forward with deep inner connect. Ikigai is a word of inner soul and leads to passion statement. So ikigai is a great dragging force for oneself. Ikigai In sync with work takes the work to the next level. Ikigai making the passion statement, is a great choice.

Ikigai has power to drag oneself out of bed in the morning. It can lead to working tirelessly and getting out of the way for work. All these stuffs are well taken by ikigai. Under all probabilities ikigai acts as a great force for this. Finding and following ikigai can be an added advantage for business and its founders. This force needs to be well harnessed and harnessed to the fullest. This provides a lot of psychological power to the business founder. This can even generate a jerk of enthusiasm. It changes the mental energy and has a positive psychological impact as well.

Beating fears

Life and fears cannot go hand in hand. One has to beat fears. This is a tough call as one has to fight with oneself. One to fight with ones thought and one's mindset. This is a self-fighting. One is expected to have a lot of setbacks and fall backs as well. The process might be long and ever going. Apart from that fighting fears, it calls for making a strong mindset as well.

The fear is a psychological factor. This further depends on circumstances and reaction to those circumstances. Most of the time fear develops before facing the circumstances as well. So, it is a reaction of psychological nature. This reaction needs to be controlled in various ways.

Fear can act as a stopper. This can stop a person from doing certain job or taking up of new assignment. Apart from professional issue fear can also lead to personal problems and health related problems. All these may be very serious in long run. All these issues are preventable if one knows how to beat the fear.

Why one need to beat fear?

Fear is a negative force. This force can do a lot of negative impact. It can even act as a hindrance and barrier. In order to know the reasons why one should fight the fear, one must know the negative impacts of fear.

1. **Hindrance and barrier:** Fear acts as a hindrance and barrier to all types of work. With the fear in mind, one cannot take up any new assignment and can even lead to improper work on existing assignment. The hindrance and barrier act as a negative force in professional life.

2. **Lack of confidence:** For all type of work, confidence is an essential factor. Lack of confidence create confusion and impacts quality of work. This also causes issue in execution of work.

3. **Health issues:** The negative force of fear creates a lot of health-related issues. Especially the mental ones. This causes a lot of lifestyle diseases as well. Such health issues are common nowadays.

4. **Inability of risk taking:** The fear and phobia prohibits a person from taking up any risk, even the calculated risks. Risk is an integral part of business. The founder must take certain calculated risk in order to carry on. Fears will lead to stopping of that.

5. **Weak decisions:** With fear in mind a founder cannot take strong decisions. He or she will always think of negative impacts of the decision taken. This will lead to weak decision making.

6. **Comfort zone mindset:** The fear will initiate the comfort zone mindset. This will stop a person from leaving the comfort zone. This can be harmful in long run.

Above mentioned six points are just of few. The list is quite long. All these situations are the impacts created by fear and phobias. It is important to beat these with strong mindset.

Below are the reasons why one need to beat the fears

1. **To get clarity of thought:** Fear overshadows one's vision and thought process. A lot of free-flowing thought gets interrupted due to fear or phobia. With fear getting under control thoughts too get free and vision gets a clarity.

2. **To start a new assignment:** The fear stops a person from taking up new assignments. So, if fear gets removed, the person's ability to take new assignment gets restored.

3. **To get a habit of calculated risk taking:** Business is all about taking risk in a calculated way. Once again, the fear acts as a big hindrance over here. With the removal of fear people can get into it in a calculated way.

4. **To get work organised:** Fear spoils the execution of work. This disrupts almost every aspect of it. Removal of fear leads to the work getting organised.

5. **To increase efficiency:** Fear hampers work efficiency. It gets drastically reduced because of fear. So, with fear removed efficiency can be regained.

6. **To have better decision making:** Fear hampers decision making to a huge extent. It even impacts the quality of decision making as well. Best quality of decision-making are always taken with fearless mind.

7. **To handle situations in a better way:** Business calls for a lot of unplanned situations which comes up. Such situations require a free and fearless mind to handle. A fearless mind can handle situation in a better

way.

8. **To get better physical and mental health:** Fear can act as a great health risk. It can lead to a lot of lifestyle and mental ailments. Removal of the fear leads to removal of health risk as well.

About eight points are just a few to quote. The benefits of fear handling are uncountable. Every people get benefited in some way or other, by conquering ones fear. This is a great lifestyle practice. Benefits will start appearing in long run and over a period of time.

Identifying one's fear

In order to fight fear, one need to identify the fears first. This at times becomes a tricky affair for a business founder. It requires deep introspection. This requires time as well. Deep introspection requires a thorough self-talk. There are many ways and theories for this. Many great personalities have suggested many techniques for this.

This process requires a lot of introspection time and patience. I am suggesting the following ten points for identifying fear.

1. **Calm your mind:** Calming the mind is very important before any task. Mind has to get uncluttered and stable. This creates your brain with a lot of energy. A cool and calm surrounding is very beneficial. Needless to say, distractions like mobile, laptop should not be there. This makes the mind ready for the mental exercise.

2. **Take pen and paper:** Best way to do any type of mental exercise is with pen and paper. One need to write down all thoughts and the flash of ideas. This is must. Many thoughts and ideas disappear within moment. Pen and paper can capture those. These are the real and powerful instruments.

3. **Think about your worries:** Once your mind is calm and you have pen and paper with you, then you start this mental exercise. First take some deep breath and take out all your thoughts other than your worries. Next is, start thinking about all matters which makes you worried. Start noting those in bullet points. You might find few points as silly ones, but that does not matter. Just keep thinking and keep writing. At the end of the exercise, you will find a lot of points which makes you worried. Repeat this exercise few more times. You will find the points which worry you, are on the paper. Go through all the points, refine them and write a quick one-line description of each

4. **Write components of worry**: After you write your worries, take up any point. Describe the worry on paper. Sub-divide that into contributing components. Every worrying point are contributed by many contributing points. These points contribute the real cause of worry.

For example, a worrying point could be "fear of loss making". It may have many contributing factors. Some are as below.

- Low sales
- High operating expenses
- Chances of penalty imposition
- High fixed cost
- Low profit margin
- Low flow of inquiry

Above six points, just for example, can contribute to the fear of loss making. Just like this a worrying factor will have a lot of contributing factors. Pinpoint the contributing factor. It is important to do so in order to find the real cause of worry.

5. **Analyse each component**: Once you have each component in place, return which contributes to your worry. Then start analysing each component. This analysis must be on contribution of those components to worry. Some components can contribute a little more and some little less. Every component has its own weightage. Impact of each component is also different. Some may have a larger impact some may have lesser impact. So, the impact analysis is also important here. These factors' weightage and impact determine the severity of the factor. Weightage and impact will vary on situation and person too.

6. **Identify which component worries you**: After analysing the weightage and impact of component, one must identify which component worries him or her more. Most of the time high impact factor makes one worried. This worrying component could become the reason of fear and stress. There could be more than one component. Even all the components can make a person worried.

7. **Describe your worry component**: Once you have identified the worry component. It is important to describe the component in detail. This description must include the points like

- Why these worries?
- How these worries?
- When this worries?
- How this factor plays a role?
- What could be the consequences of this factor?
- When may these consequences appear?
- Impact on me and business?

Above mentioned seven points can be of great help to know and understand about the fear component worrying you. This will also bring a clarity.

8. **Factors contributing to component:** Once you describe the factor, it is important to find the factors which are contributing to this component. This might require a bit of study as well. This might be bit technical in nature.

For example, reference to point number 4, if the worry component is "low flow of inquiry", then below factors could be the contributing factors:

- Low market penetration
- Improper customer approach
- Lack of marketing activities
- Improper database
- Low cold calls
- Improper product presentation
- Wrong target market

These could be numerous. Such contributing factors can have a long list. These contributing factors will give you for clarity about the factor. This factor can be real points which require workout or brainstorming.

9. **Why the component worries you:** After identifying the component that worries you and the factors contributing it you, need to do a deep analysis, why that factor worries you. But this further analysis the fear. One need to pinpoint the reason, why the component worries you. This may seem like a similar situation, as the point before but there is a fine line of difference.

For example, reference to point number 4 if the worrying component is "low flow of inquiry" the reason for warning could be

- Low revenue and materialization.
- Difficult to manage expenses.
- Issues with handling fixed expenses.
- Difficulty to manage pay-outs.
- Difficulty in managing rent payment.
- Difficulty in paying staff salary.
- Depletion of cash reserve.

There could be many more points to this. These may vary from industry to industry and from person to person.

10. **What could this lead to:** This point calls for analysis of consequences. The consequences analysis leads to full analysis of fear. Here a founder needs to analyse what components can lead to. This can further justify the fear. In other words, this is the end result of the factor.

For example, referring to point number 4 if the worrying factor is "low flow of inquiry" then the consequence could be

- Expense overshooting the revenue.
- Negative cash flow.
- Balance sheet turning negative.
- Increase in liability.
- Inability to run the business.

Above mentioned points are just for example. There could be many more points. These points are relative in nature. It varies from situation to situation and industry to industry. These points are real and actual reasons for once worry and fear.

Mindset and fear

Mindset plays a huge role in dealing with fear. This is one of the key factors. Mindset is very powerful instrument. This leads to many unexpected results at times. Mindset has amazing power. Many great personalities have nurtured this in order to get great results.

Mindset can play a huge role in dealing with fear. This makes the way for beating the fear as well. A strong mindset can face fear and deal with it in a much better way. Mindset can help of founder to lead in tough situations as well. Such situations may be disturbing for a founder, but right mindset can help to deal with it in a better way. Once you know how to face and deal with it, your fear factor gets reduced to a huge extent.

As a part of strong mindset, one need to have a positive mindset as well. In today's world, negativity is raining everywhere - in media, in social-media, in talk-shows etc. It takes a toll on everyone. This further gives rise to fears and phobias. So, this acts as a source of negative actions as well. So fighting with negativity is very important. Best way to do this is to have a positive mindset. Positive mindset is a blessing. It is an asset.

Negativity is a big barrier in journey of entrepreneurship. This has the power to stop any assignment. This defers the start. It is not only can stop but can disrupt the various processes as well. This can reduce efficiency and quality of work. A person with negative mindset can not only gets reduced to a person of doubt but also a person of low energy, low efficiency, and quality. This makes more impact in long run.

On the other hand, a positive frame of mind acts as a real blessing. This is the real motivating force. Rather I must say it is a source of self-motivation. Self-motivation is a source of abundance energy. So, **no external factor can give you any motivation unless you are self-motivated**. Mindset plays a role on this. Positive mindset can face fears and phobias in much better way. Most of the cases the fear factor is less in a person with positive mindset. The positive mindset is the right fit for challenging journey of entrepreneurship.

Setbacks and fallbacks

Setbacks or fallbacks are quite common in entrepreneurship journey. Setbacks are the phases a start-up founder has to face day in and day out. Setback maybe because of various reasons. Both the situations are inevitable. They are common and everyone face that. Setbacks and fall-back leads to fears and phobias as well. This can be treated as one of the most common sources of fear.

In business, every step is not going to work. There are more steps which will not work. Very few steps can give you affirmative results. This happens in every business. There are many steps which might work initially but have a failure in later stages. There are certain steps which might not work as well. While beating fears, setbacks and fallbacks can be great hindrances.

These are the major negativity sources which flows. Fears mainly originate in entrepreneurship journey for setups and failures. People fear failures and losses. This is how the fear factors develop.

Nurturing techniques

Mind is an amazing machine it has amazing powers. It must be well explored. So, it is important to explore the powers of the mind. This is a great way to face and fight the fear. Ancient Indian sages were known to be an expert in this. They used many techniques to explorer and exercise the power of mind. Apart from that the modern psychologist and psychiatrists too advocate various ways to nurture the mind and its powers.

I am mentioning here few techniques which can be of great help.

I. **Imagination:** This is a great technique. Imagination has a lot of power. This is a great mental exercise. This technique is well nurtured by artists and musicians. This has wonderful source of creativity. I have time and again said the mind is an amazing instrument. It can imagine the things which do not even exist. Many inventors too explored this technique.

One can use this technique to beat fears and phobias. After you have identified your phobias and related reasons. Imagine the world without it. Imagine the phobias fading away and the reasons contributing to the phobia also fades away. Give it a deep thought. Think of a world full of positivity and calmness. There is no space for negative vibes and chaos. Keep thinking a scenic which brings positiveness in your mind. May this be sunrise, sea or mountains. Imagine the work which you fear. Imagine how you want to take the next step in the swiftest way. Imagine the steps with courage and confidence. Imagine you are full of deep energy. Imagine the accomplishment of results by fulfilling the goal set. Imagine the seamless path to your goal. Imagine how seamless your work is. Imagine how the goal is achieved. Imagine the burst of positive energy. Count your blessings. Keep having deep breath.

Many creative entrepreneurs use this technique on regular basis. This also stimulates the subconscious mind. Subconscious mind has amazing power. This can drag a person to action. Imagination creates the plan in the brain. This outlines the work and the plan. Once the map of work is outlined in brain, in form of imagination, the next step gets bit easy and organised. The imagined plan and organised action can help to face phobias to a great extent. This makes the person of fear, acquainted with the forthcoming situations. This reduces the phobias to a huge extent.

II. **Determination and discipline:** Entrepreneurs are a different breed of human. They have very strong mindset. Here comes the two factors determination and discipline. These are the pillars. Determination fosters the goal. Once the start-up founder determines the goal and the target, the vision of business journey gets fostered. This is the wonderful way to set forward the plan. The determination is not easy. This requires well-defined idea and clarity of vision. Determination creates a psychological framework. This is a tool to create a favourable mindset. Most of the start-up founders struggle to set a favourable mindset for entrepreneurship journey.

Here, the determination must be well-thought. Selection of the words in determination is very important. Right words have a lot of power. Determination is a target or goal set by the founder of entrepreneur. Most of the time, it is informally done. But it is the most dragging force. The founder determines this first. This creates the steppingstone for the business journey. This journey is the foundation and starts from determination.

Discipline is the pathway to achieve the goal selected during determination phase. Discipline creates a daily ritual which takes one near to the goal. This takes one out of the bed in the morning. Drags one to the regular work to facilitate Goal chasing.

When one is full of determination and tracked by the discipline then the mind is fully engaged and occupied. This leaves no room for phobia or confusion. The two factors are the real factors which can fight all weaknesses and drive towards the goal. These are the powerful tools.

III. **Repetitions - The "japa' technique:** Ancient Indian sage were the masters of this technique. They repeated many mantras for many times. The advocated that, the ancient "japa" technique can make the mantra work. This technique is even mentioned by Dr Joseph Murphy in his book the power of your subconscious mind. Many philosophers too mentioned this technique for many benefits.

Ancient Indian sages mastered this technique. They have mastered prolonged repetitions of selected mantras. This made their mind resonate with the mantra. This attended the stage of "siddha" or perfection. This requires a lot of patience. This is a very powerful technique. This can make one believe certain points or statement. This can help a start-up founder or an entrepreneur to create a mindset. This can lead the way to amazing results.

In order to get the full benefits of this one need to make the appropriate affirmation for oneself. This must be related to the issue one is facing. I suggest below point to start the practice. This practice is well advocated by Dr Murphy in his book. This can even differ from person to person and situation to situation.

a. **Identification of the issue:** Every start-up founder has certain issues. So, clarity on the issue is important. Exact issue needs to be covered. This point required some deep analysis of the issue. This may require a lot of time at times. More the clarity, better it is. This makes the next step clear and smooth.

b. **Prepare solution with affirmation:** Once the problem is defined one need to frame and affirmation to present in form of the solution or enter result. For example, if you get nervous while making a presentation then you can make affirmation as "I am confident while making presentation". Or you can make it like this "I am comfortable and well organised while making up presentation". Such type of affirmation helps a brain to get well-versed with the positive and the right condition. These will slowly melt away the phobias and all negativities.

c. **Clear the mind:** Before you go ahead with this technique. It is very important to clear the mind. Mind has to be clear and perfect for transformation. This includes removing all negativities doubts, self-doubt, confusions et This will make the mind uncluttered and ready for the next step. If the mind is not clear and full of doubt, then it will be in a trap of negativity. So, this will make the next step very difficult. So, the first step is getting the mind uncluttered. This may be tough at times. Today the negativity is the raining like cats and dogs. News, media, social media has a lot negative stuff. These all make the mind negative. So, one's conscious effort to make the mind free from all unwanted stuff. This might not be an easy task, but regular practice and effort can be of help.

d. **Repeat regularly:** This is the next step. Once you have done the above points you have to repeat the affirmations regularly. This can be a make or break. Either you can get the best of the results or no results at all.

So, this is a very delicate point. Repetition must be done in the pre-determined affirmation. This acts as a seal of solution for the brain. This even activates the subconscious part of the brain. It is a very powerful machinery. This part of the brain is not directly affected by the conscious efforts but tickled by deep thoughts of brain. The repetition helps to make an impact on this part of the brain. Such repetitions can even make a positive impact as well. This helps a lot to deal with bad habits, negative thoughts, and phobias. Repetition acts as a powerful exercise. Repetition is an act of discipline. This makes the way for some amazing results. Let's explain the this with previously sited example. If you are nervous before a business presentation. You can repeat and affirmation – "I am confident while making presentation". Or you can even make "I am confident while making this presentation". Regular repetition of this affirmation can help to nurture the subconscious mind and to deal with this phobia. Best time to repeat or perform the exercise of "japa" is before bed-time and after waking up. Before bedtime nurtures your subconscious mind before sleep. A powerful exercise !!! After waking up your mind is fresh and ready to absorb new and positive ideas. Once again a powerful exercise !!! Both the times of the day are the high impact times. But with a regular practice you will find a positive change. This change of mind will be slow but steady. So regular practice in a disciplined way is must for success. The repetition or "japa" is a powerful and impactful tool. This must be explored to the fullest with the a disciplined routine.

e. **Feel the situation:** Situation is the key. Situation needs to be felt by the start-up founder. This feel helps to find the phobia to a great extent. This makes one to get deep into the situation. Brain has to get acquainted with the sam This is not easy. This takes a lot of time. The prime requirement for this is to keep the mind calm and quite in that situation. This takes a lot of effort. This seems almost impossible in the beginning. This takes a lot of patience. This requires a lot of practice. This is a massive mental exercise. Once your mind gets stable, it is important to dip into the situation for an analysis. This helps to know the situation. Think yourself indulged into the situation. Next is to take a part with previously mentioned techniques wherever applicable. This will help you and your subconscious to get acquainted with the situation. This part of the brain has amazing power. Most of the time, this results into a solution and if not solution, it helps to face the situation in a better way. This is a great help and boon for the start-up founders. This helps to fight the related complications as well

IV. **Silence:** Silence is a great exercise. This gives a lot of power to the brain. Silence helps to nurture the mind to a huge extent. Today we are living in the age of distractions. Here the listening capacity and concentration span got shortened. Silence can be a great help in this. Main reasons for the phobia are unstable and unsorted mind. Unsorted mind makes the situation go wild with depressing thoughts. Silence is having amazing power. It can unclutter the mind. Hal Elrod in his book "Miracle Morning" has given a lot of stress on this. He in fact has placed this in the daily practices' ritual.

Silence can lead to deep thoughts in brain. This is of immense benefit for everyone. Deep thoughts lead to solution to a lot of problems. This is just a result of uncluttered mind and thoughts. Silence leads to deep focus as well. Silence helps mind to seek solution which is generally not available.

Silence combined with deep thought sessions are great tools for start-up founders. This helps to find solution to many issues and problems. More the issues are sorted, more phobias vanish. This is a great tool. Initially it may not be easy to practice. Mind continuously wanders. This is the practice of self-control. A silent place can be an added benefit in this practice. More you practice, more your mind gets uncluttered. Most of the time our brain is in the stage of too much receiving. This process is unfiltered. This engages the brain to a huge extent. Such engagement makes one negative and confusing. This makes the brain to become over engaged. This can make one confused and fearful. Best way to counter the situation is to make the brain calm. Silence is one of the easiest ways to do so.

Silence is bit difficult to practice these days. But regular effort is the key here.

V. **Introspection:** Introspection is a great habit. It gives a thought of check for oneself. Introspection requires a lot of analytical power. Introspection is advocated by ancient Indian text in form of "swa-adhyaya". Ancient Indian sages stressed a lot on this. Introspection reveals a lot of fact about oneself. Introspection is a process which makes one aware about oneself. This has a lot of benefits. This helps to a great extent to identify one's shortcomings and faults. Moreover, if done on a regular basis, it helps to identify even small mistakes. This can help to prevent bigger mistakes. Bigger mistakes happen when the smaller mistakes go on unchecked for a long time. So, the introspection acts as a big checking point.

In order to nurture the mind, introspection plays a big role. This helps to find the pinpoints in business. This helps to find the issues which causes phobia and fear. Identification of this fear factor helps to take the prevention or curative steps.

There are different ways to take up this process. Easiest way to take up this process yes to follow the below steps

- Sit in a calm and quiet place.
- Take pen and paper with you.
- Take deep breath.
- Think on the flow of work.
- Identify any mistake or flaws.
- Note the discovery or thoughts.
- Repeat till you are satisfied.

Initially, this would be a tough one. But with a regular practice, this can start yielding results. This will help you and your brain to realise the faults and mistakes on a regular basis.

VI. **Meditation or "dhyana"**: This is a very powerful technique - powerful to the core. Ancient Indian text have mentioned about this technique thousands of years ago as "dhyana". In fact, this is considered one of the 10 factors of ancient religions. This charges a person to the fullest and pacifies the mind.

In today's world, owing to various digital distractions the human mind gets out of focus. So, lack of focus and loss of concentration is a common phenomenon. In this situation, the practice of meditation plays an important role. Meditation not only increases focus and concentration, but also makes the thoughts uncluttered. It has many health-related benefits too. It has a positive impact on anxiety, fear and hypertension. This makes a mind calm and peaceful. A calm mind is a blessing in today's world.

Initially people mind finds it difficult to practice meditation but with regular practice one can achieve this.

There are many methods of doing this. However, there are two most popular ways mentioned in ancient Indian text for this.

1. **Observer Method:** This technique directs one to be an observer of the thoughts. One has to sit in a calm place and in comfortable position. Take some slow and deep breaths. Close your eyes. Take out all your worries. Sit and remain still. Allow all thoughts to come to your mind, you be a mere observer of thoughts. Once the thought come, let it come to not stop. Let lots of thoughts keep coming. Important here is one must be conscious. Remember not to get flowed with the ongoing thoughts. Just be an observer of all thoughts. Slowly your brain will get conscious about the flow of thoughts. This will slowly make the brain stop the flow of unwanted thoughts. This process takes a lot of time and requires regular practice. This clarifies thoughts and makes the mind calm. With removal of unwanted thoughts, brain gets focused and charged. This also removes a lot of fear and confusion.

2. **Guarding Method:** This is another method of meditation. In this technique your conscious mind has to be a guard. This guard has to stop the flow of thoughts. This technique emphasises on a blank mind. Every time a thought enters your mind erase it. Make the brain blank. Again, you will find another thought entering your mind. Erase it again. Make the mind blank. Keep repeating it. With a lot of practice your mind will be able to restrict the unwanted flow of thoughts. This practice restricts the thought and keeps the mind stable. It also freezes the mind from disturbances. This form of meditation is bit advanced form, as stopping the entry of the thought require a lot of practice. It might seem bit tough at the beginning.

These two techniques can be of great help for the start-up founders. This will be able to clarify the thought and pacify the mind of a founder. Clear thought and the calm mind can help to tackle bigger obstacles as well.

VII. **The subconscious mind:** Subconscious mind is a great subject. This is one part of the brain which is not controlled by the conscious mind. This is bit complicated to understand. This part of the brain influences thoughts and thinking. It also commands the mood. But our conscious mind do not control this part of the brain. This part of the brain was well explained and described by Dr Joseph Murphy in his book "The power of Your Sub-conscious Mind". This is a great book about subconscious mind. This mind gets impacted by regular focus and work. This happens over a period of time. This is a disciplined process. One's belief plays an important role here. Subconscious mind has amazing power. Power can act as a boon for an entrepreneur. This makes the way to explorer it.

Two techniques are well known for this.

1. **Repetition**. I have already mentioned this technique previously. Repetition resonates. This resonates the subconscious mind, and the information enters there. This impacts the thinking and the work pattern. Once the subconscious mind is nurtured the impact can be seen in life
2. **Imagination**. In this technique one has to imagine with the strong conviction that target and the final result on a positive note. This will paint a picture of achievement in subconscious mind. This will affect the thoughts and actions.

Subconscious mind has a lot of power to drive a thought into action. Subconscious mind can track a person to achievement and constructive actions. This is the epicentre of motivation and encouragement. However, the subconscious mind is at double edged sword. Nurturing the sub-conscious mind to a wrong or negative role, can be very harmful for a person. So right mindset and positivity makes a difference.

These techniques can really help you to come out of fear and take up the new assignments. This can even pacify and stabilise your mind to a huge extent.

CHAPTER XII

The "Navarasa" Theory – Analysis Of Emotions

Every person on this planet is a subject of many emotions. These emotions make an impact on a person. This impact creates the behaviour of the person. Emotions are powerful factors in person's personality. Being a person, it is very important to analyse the emotion.

Every person has a lot of emotion. These are not generally created but comes naturally over a period of time. The circumstances play an impact on this. Based on the situation, emotions trigger and makes it a dominating or influencing factor.

Ancient Indian text "Natyashastra" - dedicated to form of dance- written by sage Bharat Muni, is one of the first to mention this. He termed this as "navarasa" or nine essences. Here he pointed nine types of emotions. As per the text the forms of dance, expresses the combination of these nine expressions or emotions. Even the human behaviour too gets expressed through these nine types of emotions. At the same time, there is an interesting aspect of this. Here, each emotion is given a representative colour. Each colour selection for the emotion is done with a well-planned accuracy.

Knowing and studying each of these nine emotions, helps an entrepreneur to deal with the fears and phobias to a great extent. This makes the way to beat those as well.

I am describing these nine emotions, in step-by-step manner:

1. **"Sringara" Rasa or decoration or make up:** This is the most important of all rasas. It is described as sacred, pure and worth seeing. It is an outcome of human nature. This represents the nature of being richly endowed with all desirable things. Excess of this makes a person inclined towards the desirable things. This type of emotion makes a person look for opportunities which lead to business avenues and profits. This is represented by colour **green.**

2. **"Hasya" Rasa or laughter:** This emotion referred to laughter or light-heartedness. Here two types of "hasya" are mentioned. One when a person laughs to himself and other when he or she makes another laugh. This rasa gives light-heartedness and relief. Excess impact of this causes

psychological impact and at times uncontrolled rasa leads to other get a behavioural discomfort too. Right use of this emotion leads to good sense of humour. This emotion is represented by **white** colour.

3. **"Raudra" rasa or Extreme anger:** This represents extreme anger or even violent anger. This is considered the most dangerous and violent of all emotions. This emotion gets well used during fight or a battle. This is the extreme furious state. Excess of this rasa leads to violent environment and also lifestyle related issues. Right use of this rasa helps to take control of extreme situation or repel an external attack. This assist to overcome a dangerous situation. It is also beneficial in taking charge of a chaotic situation. This emotion is represented by colour **red.**

4. **"Karuna" rasa or mercy or compassion:** This represents soft part of one's emotion. This is an essential part of personality. This is triggered by situations like suffering, sorrow or untoward incidents. Excess of this emotion makes a person emotionally soft or weak. People can take undue advantage of this type of persons. Tough or strong decision taking inability is also seen in this stage. Right use of this emotion helps to create a human bond or rapport. This emotion is represented by colour **grey**.

5. **"Bibhatsya" rasa or disgust:** This represents odious type emotion. This is triggered by seeing or hearing or filling undesired things. This gets into a psychological repulsion. This repulsion is expressed as disgust. Excess of this rasa makes one repulsive of certain things or situations. Right use of this helps to distance oneself from undesirable situations. This is represented by coloured **blue.**

6. **"Bhayankara" rasa or horror:** This rasa stands for horror or frightening. This is triggered by the situation of any extreme or any danger. This can even be due to some situation which is uncontrolled or harmful in some way or other. Excess of this emotion leads to extreme psychological distress and nervous breakdown. This can even lead to injury or hurt. Right use of this emotion can lead to the prevention of untoward incidents. This is to be presented by colour **black.**

7. **"Vira" rasa or bravery:** This emotion stands for courage or bravery. This is triggered by extreme self-confidence and determination. Excess of this emotion can lead to excess risk taking or under-estimating dangers. The right use of this emotion can lead to the taking calculated and well-planned risks. This may not refer to the physical bravery but any step of courage in any form. This is represented by colour **saffron.**

8. **"Adbhuta" rasa or wonder:** This emotion refers to surprise or amazement. This is triggered when an unexpected result comes up. Excess of this emotion leads to many unexpected situation or improper results. Right use of this emotion can lead to check the deviation of processes and check the unexpected situations. This is represented by colour **yellow**.

9. **"Shanta" rasa or peace:** This emotion refers to peace or tranquillity. This is triggered by calm, quiet and favourable situation. Excess of this emotion generally do not trigger any adverse reaction or situation. Rather excess might lead to delay in decision making. Right use of this situation could lead to well-handling a situation. This is represented by colour **white**.

These nine emotions are highlighted by ancient Indian sage "Bharat Muni". It tells about his in-depth research. All nine rasa describe almost every aspect of human behaviour. These are the nine ways of human reactions. In fact, many of the emotions are even shown by animals too. Many of these emotions are shown by pets, in response to certain situations. In other words, these are universal in nature.

Imbalance of Rasa

All emotions remain in human and gets triggered as per circumstances. Each circumstances trigger a specific emotion in a person. This varies from person to person. Under the same situation or circumstances one person triggers one emotion and other triggers the other emotion. In human "rasa" balance each other, as a rule of nature. This is the regular behaviour of human.

The real trigger comes when the dominance of one rasa goes up. Excess of one rasa or emotion changes the human behaviour. This makes a person bit more driven with that. This might be due to prevailing circumstances or due to the various psychological factors. Many times, many chemical factors too play a role. Imbalance most of the time is normal. But excess domination of an emotion is considered to be bad or unusual. This could be troublesome.

One of the main reasons of fear or phobia can be drawn down to the imbalance of emotions. This is not an easy stuff to derive. This requires a deep introspection. But with little effort this can be done. Once the behaviour of the person is introspected, the predominant rasa can be found. This can be the real cause of imbalance or deviated behaviour. Many a times imbalance do not create just phobia but also a deviated behaviour. This may appear in form of shying away, procrastination, confusion, anger etc. These types of behaviour are negative trends. These starts appearing in due course.

All these are the signs of rasa imbalance.

Rectification of emotions.

Emotions are the natural factors of human being. These are free flowing factors. So, when the emotions are ongoing then the human behaviours go likewise. But the cause of worry appears when one emotion dominates on the human personality. This results in deviated human behaviour, most of the time such deviations are situational in nature. This means certain situations trigger those. And once the situation normalises emotion too gets perfect. This is a general phenomenon. Real issue comes when it does not happen. And change in emotion goes on for a longer period. This impacts the human behaviour, work life and personal life. Such imbalance must be well noted, and immediate rectification must be encouraged.

I am suggesting here seven ways.

1. Introspection: Time and again I have stressed on the importance of introspection. This is very important step. It helps to find out the facts about various human behaviour. Introspection helps to detect the dominant emotion and reasons for this. This is more like a self-assessment. This can be done by the business founder himself.

First step to do this is, the behavioural introspection. In this one has to find what type of deviated behaviour one is having. For example, when a person has become short tempered than the anger emotion or "raudra" rasa is predominant. If the person is taking unnecessary risk, then "vira" rasa or bravery is predominant. Likewise, the introspection has to be done. The proper way of identification is the first step. There could be more than one emotions which can act as dominating.

Second step is, to ask to repeat the previous step from others. This maybe friends and family. They are the people who see you every day. So, any deviated behaviour will be noticed by them first - even before you realise. Many a times, one might not be able to identify the deviated behaviour. So, advice from friend and family can be a good step.

Third step is to ask from stakeholders. They are professionally connected people. So, any deviated behaviour could be noted by them as well.

So, with all these 3 steps, one will be able to make the right analysis of behaviour. This is a great step to know about one's behaviour. Once a deviated behaviour is identified, next step is to note those in a piece of paper. Best is to make it in two columns. One mentions the deviated behaviour and the other that dominating emotion. This even picturises the personality of a person.

2. Situational analysis: Many times, various situations trigger such kind of emotions. Such situations can be a situation to study. Situation can lead to a lot of reaction from a person. This situation can lead to one type of reaction in one person and other type of reaction in another person. This is a triggering point for a lot of reaction and triggering emotions. Under such circumstances, it is important to analyse the situations, which is triggering the emotional imbalance. Many times, an unwanted situation, triggers this. At times the stressful situation too triggers this. So, it is important to identify the situation first. So, it calls for proper analysis of the situation. One has to find the scenario or the situation which is triggering such emotional imbalances. This may be the initiation of a situation, or it could even be a situation or result of a situation. This requires a calm headed analysis.

Situations are specific and variable in nature. By this, I mean every person reacts to the situation in a specific way. For a same situation, one person can find it as a trigger point. For other, it could be a normal situation and easy going. Situation analysis helps to find this. This helps to identify the episode causing hard time. Best way to do so is, to note this in a tabular format an example given as below

Situation	What it triggers
Low sale	Triggers disappointment
High debtor	Triggers anxiety

Pic 2

This table will give you an analysis of the "situation of concern". This is the first step.

Next step is to extend the table with an additional column with corrective actions. So, the table will now look like as below

Situation	What it triggers	Corrective action
Low sale	Triggers disappointment	• Step up marketing • Initiate flexi pricing • Make proactive calls • Initiate offers
High debtor	Triggers anxiety	• Follow up • Reduce credit limit • Reduce credit period

Pic 3

This table now present situation that is triggering the emotion and corrective actions. All these add to mapping the mind of a founder and action to be taken. In other words, it has concern and the remedy both. This can be of great help.

3. The trigger point analysis: This is a very critical analysis. This refers to the point which triggers the imbalance of emotion. This is bit different from previous points. Previous point analysis the situation and this point analysis the point that triggers. This is the point in which the situation crosses the limit of tolerance and leads to imbalance of emotions. Such point of burnout leads to outburst of an imbalanced emotion. Finding out that point is the key here.

A person can bear an unfavourable situation to a limit. This comes in form of a tolerance point. Some have higher tolerance points whereas some have low tolerance point. Once that gets crossed, people start having imbalances of emotion. So, in order to handle this, it is important to have an analysis of that point.

This point is different for different people. Psychologically tough people will have this point high and vice versa. So, one has to find this triggering point.

There is no defined rule to find this point. One has to do a self-analysis, in order to get this. Apart from this, the point is a variable in nature. For one situation, the point could be low and for other situation the point could be high. So, a self-analysis can give a fair idea in this regard. Variability can always be there. Point will keep moving with situation. One need to find the point after which the emotion imbalance takes place.

Once you get that make a note of this. Once you make a note make the similar table as mentioned below

Situation	The trigger point	What it triggers	Corrective action
Low sale	Sale below $100 per day	Triggers disappointment	<ul><li>Step up marketing</li><li>Initiate flexi pricing</li><li>Make proactive calls</li><li>Initiate offers</li></ul>

Pic 4

While making this, it is important to pinpoint the precision of triggering point. That will help you to deal with it in a better way.

4. Analysis of the end result and damage by the fear factor: This is analysing of the end result of the fear factor. This is bit interesting.

Firstly, one need to find the fear factor. This can be numerous. Identification of fear factor is important for this exercise. This process might call for introspection. The identification helps to pinpoint the fear factor and its consequences.

Secondly, once you get the factor causing fear or phobia, then you have to analyse the end result if the factor is let loose. This can be the ultimate result of the factor, if left uncontrolled. The end result could lead to sowing the seed of phobia and embedded in your soul and mind.

Now this can be made in form of a table. An example as below

Fear factor	End result
Low sale	<ul><li>Low revenue</li><li>Negative cash flow</li><li>High liability</li><li>Bankruptcy and insolvency</li><li>Leading to closure</li></ul>

Pic 5

Like this you can try with all type of factors worrying you. This table will have your fear factor along with the end result.

Thirdly, analyse each factor and end result. Then categorized this as very severe, less severe and not severe. These three analyses will make your phobias get clear. All fear factors might not require your immediate attention. Some may not require your attention immediately. Some might be ignored as well. This clarifies the severity and your strategy to deal with that as well.

Fourthly, take up and work upon very severe factors, followed by less severe and not severe. This prevents your attention to get diverted and divided. You can dedicate your energy towards a specific set of factors.

This analysis opens up the opportunities to skip certain points which do not need immediate attention.

5. Ways to prevent and handle consequences: Next, one has to figure out the ways by which end result can be prevented. This exercise to be done with a lot of workouts. This step will give you the real way to fight the phobia.

If you are aware, how to handle the end result and its consequences, quite obviously your phobia slowly gets out. This is the real workout. This gives the real escape from phobia. This requires a lot of concentration and planning.

In order to make this fruitful it is recommended to have it in form of a table. The table generally has 4 columns which mentions the following points

i. **Fear factors:** This is the fear factor which one is having.
ii. **End result:** Mention of the end result if the fear factor is let loose
iii. **Precautions:** There are preventive measures which one can take to prevent the end results.
iv. **Dealing with results:** If the end result appears what steps one must take to deal with those.

The table will look as below :

Fear factor	End result	Precautions	Dealing with results
Low sale	<ul><li>Low revenue</li><li>Negative cash flow</li><li>High liability</li><li>Bankruptcy and insolvency</li><li>Leading to closure</li></ul>	<ul><li>Promotions</li><li>Flexi pricing</li><li>Sales efforts</li><li>Customization</li><li>Margin reduction</li></ul>	<ul><li>Expense reduction</li><li>Fund raising</li><li>Alternative funding</li><li>Deferred liabilities</li><li>Project deferment</li></ul>

Pic 6

This table will make you beat the phobias to the fullest as you are planning precautions and remedies together.

6. Mental exercises: Mental exercises are great way to check the emotional imbalance and phobias. These mental exercises, if done properly, have a lot of power. Best part of this is it benefits in long run. Mental exercises are undertaken by Indian sages from the time immemorial. In modern days, doctors too advocate these for many ailments.

I have described, in details, about the various mental exercises in previous chapters. Some of the ways I am mentioning here once again

First is, repetition or "japa". Repetition is a very powerful technique. This makes the subconscious mind believe about the better situation. For example, if you are angry you may repeat - I'm calm and quiet. If you are nervous, you can repeat- I'm confident. Like this you can develop your own repetition statements.

Second is meditation or dhyana. Meditation is a beneficial method to deal with such things. This explores the power of the mind to a huge extent. This is beneficial for improving concentration, dealing with anxiety and other nerve related ailments. It is an effective way of treating attention deficit disorder.

Third is imagination. This technique has a lot of impact on creativity. Many creative people have used this technique and got benefitted. Mind is an amazing machine. This takes up the technique to enhance the creativity.

Fourth is breathing exercises or "pranayama". Breathing exercises are integral part of daily rituals which ancient sages used to do. These exercises are said to pacify mind and clarify thoughts

Like this, there are many other mental exercises which can be undertaken to overcome the imbalance of emotions. These need to be done over a period of time to get the best results. These results most of the time are amazing. These can even be of benefit from various types of ailments as well.

Psychological factor and beating fear.

It is important to find the factor triggering the fear and phobia. This factor can be the real point of trigger. So, these factors can be the real stopper for all types of assignments. So, it is very important to check and keep checking this matter.

Psychological factors might seem like a very complicated stuff. But it is not. It is easy. Even a few simple self-assessment techniques can help you know about such factors. Such factor can have a lot of impact in one's behaviour and personality. Such factors require regular self-introspection as well.

In order to deal with this, one has to be in sporting spirit. At the same time, one can even go for professional help if required.

Why People Start Business ?

CHAPTER XIII

Why people start business?

Business is an interesting journey, but it is full of ups and downs. In business, people face good and bad time. They fail and they succeed. But in spite of all these people take up the risk and start business.

Question comes why?

I have noted here main reason for people starting business:

1. Idea of new product / service: Before starting any business, a person incubates the idea of a new product or a new service in his or her mind. The execution of this idea comes out in form of business. The urge to make a new product or service is irresistible. This urge paves the way for new business. This is more of a mental exercise than something on ground. Mental game is the fist game to take up in business. Here the journey is planned and made inside brain

2. Venture of own: The urge of start a venture of own drags the person towards business. Own venture is generally a dream of every person at some point of time or other. People who do so have an appetite for risk. Generally younger geeration is of notion that investing same amount of time – as invested in office – in own venture can reap more income than the salary.

3. Sense of security: In present time, unlike older time, younger generation has a sense of security prevailing. This is because a greater support from the parents or family. Their physiological needs - as per Maslow's Hierarchy of Needs – are well taken care by their parents. This make them bit secure to take risk – unlike their earlier generations. This sense of security gives them the appetite to take risk. In order other to start business.

4. Encouragement by startup schemes: Government all across globe is encouraging business and startups. This is because these ventures generate employment and contribute to economy. This step is done to increase the numbers of employment givers than increasing number of employments. This has an exponential impact.

5. Being own boss: Whenever one start business, he or she becomes own boss. This I an appealing factor. However, once the company grows and more stakeholders come, the reporting patters changes. Even owner of company becomes answerable to the stakeholders. But, even after that, this is an appealing factor.

6. Service to society: Urge to serve the society – by solving a persisting problem – drags a person to start a business. This is more of an inspirational factor. This factor dragged many entrepreneurs to start up new ventures. Srikant Bolla is a living example who started his venture to provide employment to specially abled people.

These factors make a person to start a business. This not only starts a business but makes world a better place to live.

Epilouge

The term "entrepreneur" first appeared in Jacques des Bruslons' 1723 French dictionary Dictionnaire Universel de Commerce. Entrepreneurship is a common term these days. It is commonly referred to as the process of establishing and operating a business. The term is heavily emphasised in the study of production factors in economics.

The 4 factors are

1. Land
2. Labour
3. Capital
4. Entrepreneurship

As a result, the term's popularity skyrocketed. The modern usage of the word is quite different. Now a days this is used as synonym of business. However, in practise, this word has a broader meaning. This also includes the term "startups," which is used in another context. Entrepreneurship encompasses all startup businesses.

Entrepreneurship is a tough call and requires a lot of guts as the call does not guarantee success and it is full of struggle. But the journey is also fascinating. To participate in the journey, a person places a large bet. He may quit his job, invest his savings, take out a loan, spend time, and so on. This is a risk that the entrepreneur accepts. However, it is possible that it will not be as successful. Sometimes breakeven takes longer than expected, sales do not increase, bankers refuse payment, products fail, and so on.

So patience and adequate financial backing are essential. Most aspiring entrepreneurs abandon the process after a few months, claiming that it does not pick up. No, it will not! Starting a business is similar to giving birth to a child. Baby will mature and begin to crawl, stand, walk, and eventually run. All of this takes time. Meanwhile, proper financial management, sales growth, cost control, vendor management, maintaining quality, and so on are all equally important. It is not going to be easy. It is the ultimate journey. Millions begin the journey, many abandon it, many fail, and only a few succeed. It's just like any other line of work. It's similar to playing cricket. Almost everyone plays, but only a few make it to the professional level, and only one wins the World Cup. This is the same journey.

Entrepreneurship is an amalgamation of art, science, and commerce. This is genuine bootstrapping. You must complete all tasks correctly, from office opening to closing. Nothing can be said "NO" to. This is how one brand is constructed. Everything big starts small. As a result, the smaller the start, the lower the risk. Most people make the mistake of starting large. Yes, I agree that the magnitude of the leap could be enormous due to the large start. However, the risk grows exponentially. As a result, it is always preferable to begin small and then leapfrog the growth curve.

Overall, entrepreneurship is a difficult but exciting journey!

9 789888 951301 8